# NANCY JO SULLIVAN

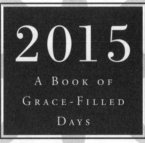

# 2015

## A BOOK OF
## GRACE-FILLED
## DAYS

D1457062

A JESUIT MINISTRY

Chicago

# LOYOLA PRESS.
## A JESUIT MINISTRY

3441 N. Ashland Avenue
Chicago, Illinois 60657
(800) 621-1008
www.loyolapress.com

Cover and interior design by Kathy Kikkert.

ISBN-13: 978-0-8294-3993-9
ISBN-10: 0-8294-3993-5
Library of Congress Control Number: 2014936771

Printed in the United States of America.

14 15 16 17 18 19 Bang 10 9 8 7 6 5 4 3 2 1

# INTRODUCTION

Last spring, on a warm April morning, I began writing the devotional that you now hold in your hands. It wasn't the ideal time to write a book, that's for sure. I had just moved into a new home, a little cottage near a lake. Now my living room was brimming with cardboard boxes, a treadmill, and furniture piled with trinkets and books. Leaning against my refrigerator were the pieces to my dining-room table. My future office, a small den, was lined with empty bookshelves and framed photos of my grown children.

As the sun streamed through the windows above the fireplace, I pulled an official looking book from a backpack: the Lectionary. Setting the sacred book on top of a box, I pulled up a stepstool. For now this was my office space. As I thumbed through the pages, I felt overwhelmed.

This wasn't just any book. It was a carefully measured collection of readings, a calendar of holy days and seasons, and a celebration of saints and solemnities.

A few months earlier, I had signed a contract with Loyola Press. With just one signature, I had made a promise to my publisher. I would use the Lectionary prayerfully and carefully. In approximately six months, I would write 365 reflections, one for each day of the church year.

"Oh my," I said now, in the clutter. How could I write what I needed to write? My computer wasn't even hooked up. In this abyss of my disordered home, how could God speak? "Lord, send your spirit. From the chaos, organize my thoughts and words. Show me where to begin." I began digging into a nearby box and unearthed a pen and paper.

That day, as I sat amid my boxed belongings, I wrote four reflections for Advent. The next day, another four. Over the course of many weeks, four reflections a day turned into 40, 80, and 100 reflections.

In between painting walls and putting away dishes, I wrote on legal pads, scrap paper, and the back of paper bags. As I carried boxes to the garage, I would find myself pondering the Lectionary readings. Lost in thought, I would craft ideas in my head. Often I would hear myself whisper: *That would be a great story for Lent. Maybe I could use that idea for a feast day.*

At night, the Lectionary was always on top of my dresser. Though my headboard was leaning against the closet and my mattress was on the floor, the Lord's presence

filled my unorganized space. Sometimes, in the dimness of a
nightlight, I would open the Lectionary and read the words
of a Gospel or the verses of a Psalm. "Lord, what do you
want to say?" I would ask. Then, as I picked up my pen,
another reflection would come to life.

When the summer came, I often took breaks from
organizing my cottage. As I relaxed by the shoreline of
a nearby lake, I would unzip my bag and pull out the
Lectionary. While children played on a nearby playground,
I would reflect upon the scriptures and write down my
thoughts in a journal. "Lord, how does this sound?" I would
ask as sentences began taking shape on the page.

By the time I got to reflection number 360, the leaves in
my back yard were beginning to change color. One Sunday
afternoon, as I curled up on the living room couch, I began
writing the last few reflections in cursive. Lost in thought,
I looked out the window. The leaves were falling to the
ground, each one sparkling in the golden light.

I was filled with gratitude. The devotional was almost
done. How did this happen? In the abyss of a major move,
God had hovered over my life. Though the last few months
had been filled with disorder, the Lord had breathed life

into my humble thoughts and words. My prayer was simple: "Thanks Lord."

These days, my little cottage is pretty organized. My bedroom is a restful retreat, and I can bake cookies in my kitchen. Now, I often tap the keys of my laptop in my home office.

Though I would've preferred to write *Grace-Filled Days* in a calmer season of life, I've learned some very important lessons of faith. God is present in the disorder that so often defines our days. In the clutter, his voice can still be heard. If we open our hearts to his word, he will speak.

My name is Nancy Jo Sullivan. May these reflections fill your days with grace.

*Yet, O LORD, you are our father; / we are the clay and you the potter;*
*we are all the work of your hands.*
—ISAIAH 64:7

God is the master potter. Each day he is at work, molding
us into vessels that contain his power and presence. How is
God molding you? Is he using a person or situation to
shape you into his likeness? Is he bringing forth beauty
from the mud of your sin and guilt? Is he sculpting your
hurts into hope?

On this first Sunday of Advent, give God your life. Watch
God create a masterpiece from the muck and mire. Wait·
for the beauty to emerge.

Isaiah 63:16b–17, 19b; 64:2–7
Psalm 80:2–3, 15–16, 18–19 (4)
1 Corinthians 1:3–9
Mark 13:33–37

# DECEMBER 1

*O house of Jacob, come, / let us walk in the light of the LORD.*
—ISAIAH 2:5

When I pray, I often light a candle. The flame brings great comfort, especially when I am waiting on God to answer a specific prayer. The light calms my heart and beckons me to be still. In the glow, I feel that all will be well. As Advent begins, let the presence of Christ shine in you, with you, and through you. Be warmed by the glow of Christ's love. Walk in the light of the Lord.

Isaiah 2:1–5
Psalm 122:1–2, 3–4b, 4cd–5, 6–7, 8–9
Matthew 8:5–11

# DECEMBER 2

*Turning to the disciples in private, he said, "Blessed are the eyes that see what you see."*
—LUKE 10:23

Every morning, I jog through our neighborhood. Often, I pass two elderly women walking arm in arm. It's obvious that one of the women is blind; her gaze is completely unfocused. Nonetheless, they stroll merrily, talking and laughing. Yesterday, I saw them pause at a rosebush. "The roses look like wine," the seeing woman said. I watched as she picked a flower for her companion. Their friendship was wondrous to behold.

During these Advent days, watch for beautiful sights. Let your eyes be blessed.

Isaiah 11:1–10
Psalm 72:1–2, 7–8, 12–13, 17
Luke 10:21–24

# *Wednesday*

# DECEMBER 3

*Great crowds came to him, having with them the lame, the blind, the deformed, the mute, and many others. They placed them at his feet, and he cured them.*
—MATTHEW 15:30

In this season of waiting, take time to sit at the feet of Jesus. As you settle into his presence, close your eyes. Let him cure the hidden deformities in your life: bitterness, envy, unforgiveness. Wait for his healing touch.

Isaiah 25:6–10a
Psalm 23:1–3a, 3b–4, 5, 6
Matthew 15:29–37

# DECEMBER 4

• ST. JOHN OF DAMASCUS, PRIEST AND DOCTOR OF THE CHURCH •

*Trust in the LORD forever! / For the LORD is an eternal Rock.*
—ISAIAH 26:4

There's a statue of the Blessed Mother in my mom's garden. It's crafted from solid stone and has weathered more than a decade of storms and scorching heat. This lawn decoration is rock solid, just as Mary's faith was. She said yes to God, even though one day she would stand in a windstorm of grief, before the cross of her beloved son.

Are you standing before a cross? Don't budge. Stand firmly, just as Mary did. The Lord, your rock, is with you.

Isaiah 26:1–6
Psalm 118:1 and 8–9, 19–21, 25–27a
Matthew 7:21, 24–27

# DECEMBER 5

*"Do you believe that I can do this?" "Yes, Lord," they said to him.*
—MATTHEW 9:28

When the doctors told me that my daughter had just two
years to live, I prayed: "Lord, I believe that you can heal
her." But as time passed, it became clear that there would
be no physical healing. Yet as I surrendered my child's
health to God, something amazing happened. I began
thanking God for the gift of her life. *Lord, you will be with us
through all that lies ahead . . . Yes, Lord . . . I believe.* That prayer
got me through some of the hardest moments of my faith
journey. Maybe this Advent you are in a great struggle. Try
praying a small prayer that holds great power: *Yes, Lord,
I believe.*

Isaiah 29:17–24
Psalm 27:1, 4, 13–14
Matthew 9:27–31

*He tells the number of the stars; / he calls each by name.*
—PSALM 147:4

Did you know that you can name a star in honor of someone you love? Yes, for a small fee, your loved one can be immortalized forever! It sounds like the perfect gift. But

God has already named every star that shines in our universe. Try to take some long evening walks this Advent. Look up and let your eyes scan the lights that twinkle in the darkness. Stand in awe of the God who names stars.

Isaiah 30:19–21, 23–26
Psalm 147:1–2, 3–4, 5–6
Matthew 9:35–10:1, 5a, 6–8

# DECEMBER 7

• SECOND SUNDAY OF ADVENT •

*"A voice of one crying out in the desert: / 'Prepare the way of the Lord, make straight his paths.'"*
—MARK 1:3

Whenever I entertain guests, I clean my house. I scrub the floors, vacuum the carpets, and dust the furniture. Sometimes I even buy new towels for the bathroom. Cleaning house is one way to make visitors feel special. Advent is a time to tidy up our hearts, a season to prepare for the most special guest of all: Jesus. Will you be ready for his arrival?

Isaiah 40:1–5, 9–11
Psalm 85:9–10, 11–12, 13–14 (8)
2 Peter 3:8–14
Mark 1:1–8

# DECEMBER 8

*Mary said, "Behold, I am the handmaid of the Lord."*
—LUKE 1:38

When Mary became pregnant by the Holy Spirit, she faced great uncertainty. Her relationship with Joseph was imperiled. In fact, her very life was at risk; in those days, adultery was punishable by death. But through Mary, the gift of Jesus was given to the world. As you journey through these days of Advent, consider how God is calling you to say yes. What will that yes require of you? Will it bring you closer to God?

Genesis 3:9–15, 20
Psalm 98:1, 2–3ab, 3cd–4
Ephesians 1:3–6, 11–12
Luke 1:26–38

*Then the glory of the LORD shall be revealed.*
—ISAIAH 40:5

I live a few miles from the grand Cathedral of St. Paul. I often visit the holy space, just to sit and pray. I love being surrounded by sacred artwork, statues of great saints, and brightly burning votive candles. But I know God's glory cannot be contained in a cathedral. When we share a hug, receive a word of encouragement, or offer the gift of forgiveness, the glory of the Lord is revealed. During these days of Advent, be on the lookout for God's glory.

Isaiah 40:1–11
Psalm 96:1–2, 3 and 10ac, 11–12, 13
Matthew 18:12–14

*Wednesday*

# DECEMBER 10

*They that hope in the LORD will renew their strength.*
—ISAIAH 40:31

Hope. Most of us have felt it at one time or another. But few of us have described it as well as the great poet Emily Dickinson:

"Hope" is the thing with feathers—
That perches in the soul—
And sings the tune without the words—
And never stops—at all—

Quiet your heart. In the stillness, imagine a little bird perched in your soul. Listen to the bird sing. Hear the tune without words, the sacred song of hope.

Isaiah 40:25–31
Psalm 103:1–2, 3–4, 8 and 10
Matthew 11:28–30

# DECEMBER 11

• ST. DAMASUS I, POPE •

*I am the LORD, your God, / who grasp your right hand; / It is I who*
*say to you, "Fear not, / I will help you."*
—ISAIAH 41:13

The other day, as I walked into the grocery store, I saw a
young dad clutching the hand of his small son. As cars
drove past, the dad scooped the child into his arms. "Hey
there, Buddy, you've gotta stay close to me," he said. God
is like that dad. When we walk through treacherous
moments, he holds our hand tightly. Sometimes, when life
becomes too much to bear, he carries us and reminds us to
stay close.

Isaiah 41:13–20
Psalm 145:1 and 9, 10–11, 12–13ab
Matthew 11:11–15

*God's temple in heaven was opened, and the ark of his covenant could be seen in the temple.*
—REVELATION 11:19

There are definitely times when God allows lightning bolts to flash. When we lose a job, face an illness, or endure an unexpected loss, we are jolted. Though a spiritual jolt can be shocking, it can illuminate our hearts in a way nothing else can. One flash of divine light can lead us to great transformation. When have you had a lightning-bolt experience? How did it change you?

Zechariah 2:14–17 or Revelation 11:19a;
12:1–6a, 10ab
Judith 13:18bcde, 19
Luke 1:26–38 or Luke 1:39–47

# DECEMBER 13

• ST. LUCY, VIRGIN AND MARTYR •

*O shepherd of Israel, hearken.*
—PSALM 80:2

*The Lord is my shepherd; there is nothing that I lack . . .* "Can you repeat that for me?" I asked my daughter with Down syndrome. I was helping twelve-year-old Sarah memorize Psalm 23. She stuttered each word slowly and carefully: "The L-l-lord is-is m-my sh-sh-shepherd." I imagined Jesus standing over us, robed in white, staff in hand. It was a sacred moment, one that still brings me peace even though Sarah is now in heaven. *The Lord is my shepherd.* Today, say those words slowly and carefully. Draw near to the shepherd of your soul.

Sirach 48:1–4, 9–11
Psalm 80:2ac and 3b, 15–16, 18–19
Matthew 17:9a, 10–13

*May the God of peace make you perfectly holy.*
—1 THESSALONIANS 5:23

I feel the most anxiety when I have an endless to-do list. Sometimes I need to ask myself: *Are my goals unrealistic? Is there a way I can renegotiate my schedule? Can I manage my time better?* Life gets pretty busy. With so many places to go and things to do, we can easily forget that God wants us to live in peace. Have no anxiety at all, the Scriptures tell us. Today, prayerfully evaluate your daily schedule. How can you best use your time for what really matters?

Isaiah 61:1–2a, 10–11
Luke 1:46–48, 49–50, 53–54
1 Thessalonians 5:16–24
John 1:6–8, 19–28

*Monday*

# DECEMBER 15

*Your ways, O LORD, make known to me; / teach me your paths.*
—PSALM 25:4

A few years back, I was trying to determine whether I should leave my day job to pursue a writing and speaking career. I asked God to show me his will: "Give me a sign." I didn't get a visit from an angel, and there were no prophetic dreams or apparitions. The only sign I received was a strong sense that I was being called to write. I followed my heart and wrote a book. Yes, finances were tight, but the peace I gained was indescribable. Sometimes the Lord simply whispers his will to our heart. Are you listening?

Numbers 24:2–7, 15–17a
Psalm 25:4–5ab, 6 and 7bc, 8–9
Matthew 21:23–27

# DECEMBER 16

*Jesus said to the chief priests and the elders of the people: "What is your opinion?"*
—MATTHEW 21:28

When you think of God, do you imagine him valuing your opinion? When you pray, do your offer God your thoughts and ideas? Do you share your hopes and dreams? Do you believe that Jesus wants to hear the ponderings of your heart? Go ahead: talk with God. Share everything you are thinking and feeling. Imagine God asking, "What is your opinion?"

Zephaniah 3:1–2, 9–13
Psalm 34:2–3, 6–7, 17–18, 19 and 23
Matthew 21:28–32

# DECEMBER 17

*He crouches like a lion recumbent, / the king of beasts.*
—GENESIS 49:9

In the book series *Chronicles of Narnia*, Susan and Lucy ask
Mr. Beaver to tell them about Aslan, the lion who
represents a Christ figure. "Is he quite safe?" Susan asks.
"Safe?" responds Mr. Beaver. "Of course he isn't safe. But he
is good. He's the king I tell you." Following God isn't
always safe. But the great Lion of Heaven is always with us.
He roars against the dangers we face; his thunderous growl
can bring all evil to a halt. He is a protective beast, the
king of goodness and love. When have you heard the
roar of God?

Genesis 49:2, 8–10
Psalm 72:1–2, 3–4ab, 7–8, 17
Matthew 1:1–17

# DECEMBER 18

*"'And they shall name him Emmanuel,'" / which means "God with us."*
—MATTHEW 1:23

Last December, I was working on a manuscript in a coffee shop. Right next to me was an elderly woman, all alone, drinking a cup of tea. As I worked, I watched another older woman draw near to her table. "May I join you?" she asked. For the next hour, the two of them talked and laughed. "It's so nice to have some company," I heard one of them say. As Christmas approaches, make room for Emmanuel. Pull up a chair for him, let him keep you company.

Jeremiah 23:5–8
Psalm 72:1–2, 12–13, 18–19
Matthew 1:18–25

*Both were righteous in the eyes of God, observing all the commandments*
*and ordinances of the Lord blamelessly.*
—LUKE 1:6

What commandment is hardest for you to follow? For me,
honoring the Sabbath has been an ongoing challenge. But
lately I've been disciplining myself to be lazy on Sunday
afternoons. I've taken the time to lounge on the couch,
reading books and watching movies with my daughters.
Last Sunday, I actually made homemade spaghetti. I'm
finally beginning to understand why God mandated rest.
Slowing down is good for the soul.

Today is the last Friday before Christmas. How will you
spend it?

Judges 13:2–7, 24–25a
Psalm 71:3–4a, 5–6ab, 16–17
Luke 1:5–25

# DECEMBER 20

*But she was greatly troubled at what was said.*
—LUKE 1:29

It's easy to understand why the greeting of an angel would trouble Mary. She was just a teenage girl. We can only imagine what went through her mind when Gabriel began talking to her. *Full of grace? Me? I'm barely a woman.* But she had been chosen to bear the Son of God. She was troubled, but God blessed her with a great gift: courage. *May it be done unto me according to your word . . .*

Are you feeling troubled by a divine call? Be at peace. Like Mary, you will receive the courage you need.

Isaiah 7:10–14
Psalm 24:1–2, 3–4ab, 5–6
Luke 1:26–38

*But Mary said to the angel, "How can this be, since I have no relations with a man?"*
—LUKE 1:34

As we ponder Mary's encounter with Gabriel, we might remember Joseph, the righteous man who was betrothed to Mary. Though Mary became pregnant by the power of the Holy Spirit, Joseph put aside his ego and listened to the Holy Spirit. We know from Luke's next chapter that Joseph took Mary as his wife. He lovingly raised the offspring of God—a son who wasn't his. If you want to be righteous, follow Joseph's example. Surrender your life to God's purposes.

2 Samuel 7:1–5, 8b–12, 14a, 16
Psalm 89:2–3, 4–5, 27, 29 (2a)
Romans 16:25–27
Luke 1:26–38

# DECEMBER 22

"My soul proclaims the greatness of the Lord; / my spirit rejoices in
God my savior."
—LUKE 1:46

When Mary traveled to Elizabeth's home, it was a long
trip, about a hundred miles over rugged terrain. On that
journey, she would've had a lot of time to think, maybe
even worry. She might have wondered, *Who will believe that
my child is God's Son?* Yet when she arrived at her cousin's
home, she was able to say, "My soul proclaims the
greatness of the Lord; and my spirit rejoices in God my
savior." As Christmas draws near, let Mary's words become
the song of your heart. Don't worry about anything;
instead, proclaim the greatness of the Lord.

1 Samuel 1:24–28
1 Samuel 2:1, 4–5, 6–7, 8abcd
Luke 1:46–56

*When the time arrived for Elizabeth to have her child she gave birth to a son.*
—LUKE 1:57

Not one of my three children arrived on the "due date." On the contrary, I began to feel labor pains a week before or a few days after the dates calculated by our doctor. Our babies were born when they were ready to be born. Their first cries were heard at a time appointed by God. Sometimes we want God to give us an exact time when he will act: a due date. But God's plan always unfolds at just the right time, as St. Elizabeth knew well. Are you waiting for God to do something? Be patient.

Malachi 3:1–4, 23–24
Psalm 25:4–5ab, 8–9, 10 and 14
Luke 1:57–66

*Wednesday*

# DECEMBER 24

*"The dawn from on high shall break upon us, / to shine on those who dwell in darkness and the shadow of death."*
—LUKE 1:78–79

In this season of hope, let us remember those who are grieving. In their anguish, they dwell in the darkness of pain and loss. For them, the shadow of death veils the light of Christmas joy. As you prepare to welcome Jesus into your heart, call to mind all those who have lost a loved one this past year. Let your prayers shine on them.

MORNING:
2 Samuel 7:1–5, 8b–12, 14a, 16
Psalm 89:2–3, 4–5, 27 and 29
Luke 1:67–79

# DECEMBER 25

• THE NATIVITY OF THE LORD (CHRISTMAS) •

*For a child is born to us, a son is given us; / upon his shoulder*
*dominion rests. / They name him Wonder-Counselor, God-Hero, /*
*Father-Forever, Prince of Peace.*
—ISAIAH 9:5

On this Christmas Day, the Scriptures invite us to ponder
the names of God, who is our counselor, a pastoral
presence who understands the secrets of our heart. Our
Savior is a valiant hero, one who rescues us from danger.
With great mercy and tenderness, the God we serve is a
loving father. Regal and glorious, our Lord wears the
shimmering crown of a king. On the birthday of Jesus,
which of God's names speaks to you?

VIGIL:
Isaiah 62:1–5
Psalm 89:4–5, 16–17, 27, 29 (2a)
Acts 13:16–17, 22–25
Matthew 1:1–25 or 1:18–25

DURING THE NIGHT:
Isaiah 9:1–6
Psalm 96:1–2, 2–3, 11–12, 13
Titus 2:11–14
Luke 2:1–14

DAWN:
Isaiah 62:11–12
Psalm 97:1, 6, 11–12
Titus 3:4–7
Luke 2:15–20

DAY:
Isaiah 52:7–10
Psalm 98:1, 2–3, 3–4, 5–6 (3c)
Hebrews 1:1–6
John 1:1–18 or 1:1–5, 9–14

*Stephen, filled with grace and power, was working great wonders and signs among the people.*
—ACTS 6:8

St. Stephen performed great miracles. He was martyred for his faith, and before he died, he saw a vision of heaven. If we compare ourselves to this spiritual giant, we might feel a bit insecure in our faith life. But Mother Teresa is regarded as having said, "Not all of us can do great things. But we can do small things with great love." Today, do *something*—with great love.

Acts 6:8–10; 7:54–59
Psalm 31:3cd–4, 6 and 8ab, 16bc and 17
Matthew 10:17–22

*Be glad in the LORD.*
—PSALM 97:12

Did you know that there are two different kinds of smiles? A fake smile is not attached to any specific emotion; it involves only the muscles around the mouth. A true and intentional smile causes all the muscles around the eyes to crinkle (psychologists call this a Duchenne smile). What about your smile? Take up this challenge today: "Be glad in the Lord." Then stand in front of a mirror. You might just see crinkles around your eyes.

1 John 1:1–4
Psalm 97:1–2, 5–6, 11–12
John 20:1a, 2–8

*Now, Master, you may let your servant go / in peace, according to your word, / for my eyes have seen your salvation.*
—LUKE 2:29–30

All of us will come to the last moment of our lives. Will we make our way to eternity filled with the comfort of Christ and the peace of a well-lived life? When we arrive at the gates of heaven, will we hear the Lord say, "Well done, good and faithful servant"? Let us use wisely every moment.

Sirach 3:2–6, 12–14 or Genesis 15:1–6; 21:1–3
Psalm 105:1–2, 3–4, 5–6, 8–9 (7a, 8a) or
Psalm 128:1–2, 3, 4–5
Colossians 3:12–21 or 3:12–17 or
Hebrews 11:8, 11–12, 17–19
Luke 2:22–40 or 2:22, 39–40

# DECEMBER 29

• ST. THOMAS BECKET, BISHOP AND MARTYR •

*"Lord, now let your servant go in peace; / your word has been fulfilled."*
—LUKE 2:29

A few years back, our parish priest stood on the altar and asked a question I've never forgotten: "What would you be willing to die for?" Thomas Becket died for his beliefs. I would die to protect my family. What do you think is worth dying for?

1 John 2:3–11
Psalm 96:1–2a, 2b–3, 5b–6
Luke 2:22–35

# DECEMBER 30

*[She] worshiped night and day with fasting and prayer.*
—LUKE 2:37

My sister Annie spends two hours each day praying.
Sometimes, when she's having a sleepless night, she'll get
up and kneel before a cross in her living room. There, she
quietly offers intercessions. During the hours after
midnight, Annie never tosses and turns. Instead, she has a
beautiful conversation with her Lord. The next time you
can't sleep, try to pray.

1 John 2:12–17
Psalm 96:7–8a, 8b–9, 10
Luke 2:36–40

# DECEMBER 31

• ST. SYLVESTER I, POPE •

*In the beginning was the Word, / and the Word was with God, / and the Word was God.*
—JOHN 1:1

Before I write, I always turn to the Scriptures. I need to know that the Author of Life, the Word, is guiding my work. As I ponder the sacred writings, I ask God to breathe his life into me. God's word is my wellspring of inspiration. How does the word of God influence your work?

1 John 2:18–21
Psalm 96:1–2, 11–12, 13
John 1:1–18

*The LORD let his face shine upon you, and be gracious to you!*
—NUMBERS 6:26

I grew up in a large Irish Catholic family. Above our front door hung the words of an Irish blessing from the book of Numbers: *May the Lord bless you and keep you; May the Lord make his face shine upon you and be gracious to you; May the Lord turn his face toward you and give you peace.* That blessing has stayed with me for decades. Sometimes, when I'm struggling with a problem, I think of God's face turning toward me. Just the thought of God watching over me brings great comfort. Are you in need of a blessing? Imagine God's face turning your way.

Numbers 6:22–27
Psalm 67:2–3, 5, 6, 8 (2a)
Galatians 4:4–7
Luke 2:16–21

*Friday*

# JANUARY 2

• SS. BASIL THE GREAT AND GREGORY NAZIANZEN, BISHOPS AND
DOCTORS OF THE CHURCH •

*As for you, the anointing that you received from him remains in you.*
—1 JOHN 2:27

If you were baptized, the sign of the cross was traced on
your forehead. "I claim you for Christ our Savior," the
priest proclaimed. As a child of God, you were also
anointed with the oil of salvation and the water of new life.
The anointing you received at baptism can never be lost.
Take a moment today to look in the mirror. Imagine the
cross that was once traced on your forehead. What does it
mean to you today to be "anointed"?

1 John 2:22–28
Psalm 98:1, 2–3ab, 3cd–4
John 1:19–28

*Saturday*

# JANUARY 3

• THE MOST HOLY NAME OF JESUS •

*See what love the father has bestowed on us.*
—1 JOHN 3:1

I live just a few blocks from a beautiful lake. During the
hot Minnesota summers, I often meet my daughters there.
As we walk the pathways that line the shore, we catch up
on news and concerns. Surrounded by a canopy of trees,
we can hear the clanging of sailboats bobbing in the water.
Butterflies flit past, and the fragrance of roses drifts
through the air. "God made all of this for our pleasure,"
I often say. If you want to experience the presence of the
heavenly Father, take a walk through nature.

1 John 2:29–3:6
Psalm 98:1, 3cd–4, 5–6
John 1:29–34

⇒ 35 ⇐

*Sunday*

# JANUARY 4

• THE EPIPHANY OF THE LORD •

*Rise up in splendor, Jerusalem! Your light has come, / the glory of the Lord shines upon you.*
—ISAIAH 60:1

When my three daughters were little, all of them were afraid of the dark. One day I bought a night-light at the hardware store, a little plastic Jesus. Maybe this would ease their fears. That night, just before bedtime, I plugged the light into an outlet in the hallway. My little girls gathered around the glowing image of God. Rachael, my youngest, was awestruck: "Mom, Jesus is shining!" After that, they slept soundly. Whatever fear you face today, remember that Jesus is shining.

Isaiah 60:1–6
Psalm 72:1–2, 7–8, 10–11, 12–13
Ephesians 3:2–3a, 5–6
Matthew 2:1–12

*"[T]he people who sit in darkness have seen a great light, / on those dwelling in a land overshadowed by death / light has arisen."*
—MATTHEW 4:16

When do you find yourself preferring darkness? Can you make some changes that will lead you to the light of Christ?

1 John 3:22–4:6
Psalm 2:7bc–8, 10–12a
Matthew 4:12–17, 23–25

*When Jesus saw the vast crowd, his heart was moved with pity for*
*them, for they were like a sheep without a shepherd.*
—MARK 6:34

After my divorce, it felt as though I was wearing an invisible *D* on my forehead. Every Sunday, when I worshipped at Mass, I sat alone in the back row. Surrounded by a sea of families, I felt distant from God. How could the Lord possibly love me? But as time passed, that pew in the back row became a place of healing. I kept hearing God say, "I love you just as you are. Thank you for coming." Maybe you find yourself sitting in the back row of guilt and shame. Let today's Scripture bring to mind the sacred heart of Jesus, that heart that is "moved with pity" for those he loves.

1 John 4:7–10
Psalm 72:1–2, 3–4, 7–8
Mark 6:34–44

*Wednesday*

# JANUARY 7

• ST. RAYMOND OF PEÑAFORT, PRIEST •

*And his love is brought to perfection in us.*
—1 JOHN 4:17

It sounds cliché, but love is what makes life beautiful. We may not have health, wealth, or a good retirement plan. But if we have the love of family, friends, and God, we are rich indeed. Today, try not to worry about the future. God will take care of that. Embrace all the love in your life.

1 John 4:11–18
Psalm 72:1–2, 10, 12–13
Mark 6:45–52

# JANUARY 8

*And all spoke highly of him and were amazed at the gracious words that came from his mouth.*
—LUKE 4:22

I know someone who always complains—about family, the government, the overgrown garden, the garbage man, the dog who barks next door—the list goes on and on. I try to avoid spending time with this person because of the negativity it brings to my life. But God keeps telling me, "Be a witness, speak to this person about me." In today's Gospel, we remember the gracious words that came out of the mouth of Jesus. Let us combat the negativity in our world by sharing the gracious words of Christ.

1 John 4:19–5:4
Psalm 72:1–2, 14 and 15bc, 17
Luke 4:14–22a

# JANUARY 9

*But he would withdraw to deserted places to pray.*
—LUKE 5:16

When I was in my mid-twenties, I attended a silent retreat.
Most of the retreatants were women in their fifties and
sixties; immediately, I felt out of place. There was no
conversation. Everyone took long walks in a quiet garden.
Holy music was always playing. I left after just a few hours.
Now that I'm in my fifties, I understand why silent prayer
is so important. From time to time, we need to withdraw
from the noise of life. When we stroll through quiet
gardens, it's easier to hear God's voice. Is God calling you
to a deserted place? If so, don't leave before he has a
chance to speak.

1 John 5:5–13
Psalm 147:12–13, 14–15, 19–20
Luke 5:12–16

# JANUARY 10

*We have this confidence in him that if we ask anything according to his will, he hears us.*
—1 JOHN 5:14

After my daughter died, it was hard to pray. My days consisted of sleeping and walking around in a daze. I grew used to feeling depressed. "This must be God's will," I told myself. Six years later, I'm experiencing a series of answered prayers. And I'm a little shocked by it all. I've moved into a cottage that is surrounded by flowers and sunlit windows. I'm speaking in public about grief, grace, and healing. I've made a host of new friends. It's been a while since I felt this kind of joy. I still don't know if suffering is God's plan. But I'm certain that God wants each of us to feel joy. It's up to us to accept the gift.

1 John 5:14–21
Psalm 149:1–2, 3–4, 5 and 6a and 9b
John 3:22–30

*A smoldering wick he shall not quench.*
—ISAIAH 42:3

A little bit of hope is like a small flame, barely flickering.
But God promises that he will never quench a smoldering
wick. So don't give up. Even a spark of hope can turn into
a roaring fire of faith.

Isaiah 55:1–11 or Isaiah 42:1–4, 6–7
Isaiah 12:2–3, 4bcd, 5–6 (3) or
Psalm 29:1–2, 3–4, 3, 9–10 (11b)
1 John 5:1–9 or Acts 10:34–38
Mark 1:7–11

# JANUARY 12

*Jesus said to them, "Come after me, and I will make you fishers of men."*
—MARK 1:17

When I was a little girl, I often went fishing for walleye with my dad. The two of us would sit in a small boat for hours, our poles dangling in the lake. Sometimes, Dad would catch scary-looking bullheads. "Dang it!" he would say, as he tossed the whiskered fish back in the water. In today's Gospel, Jesus tells us that we must be fishers of people. While it's nice to "catch" someone who is open to the Gospel, Jesus wants us to fish for the bullheaded people of the world, the ones who need him most.

Hebrews 1:1–6
Psalm 97:1 and 2b, 6 and 7c, 9
Mark 1:14–20

*"What is man that you are mindful of him, / or the son of man that you care for him?"*
—HEBREWS 2:6

My sister Annie is comical when it comes to matters of faith. Once, when she received an unexpected answer to prayer, she called and said, "I feel like a scruffy dog that has just been given a treat." My sister went on to describe herself as a shaggy mutt with wide eyes and floppy ears. "I should be barking for joy," she said, laughing. "But all I can do is tilt my head toward heaven and say, 'Me? A treat?'" But the Lord cares for us, even in our scruffy, undeserving moments.

Hebrews 2:5–12
Psalm 8:2ab and 5, 6–7, 8–9
Mark 1:21–28

# JANUARY 14

*He approached, grasped her hand, and helped her up.*
—MARK 1:31

When have you felt the hand of God in your life? I felt his
touch a few years ago, when I was attending a prayer
meeting. I was sitting alone, and the worshippers who
surrounded me began praising God. I couldn't enter the
celebration; I was struggling with a problem that seemed to
have no answer. But then I felt the presence of someone
standing behind me. As an elderly hand reached out for
mine, I heard a woman's voice: "Whatever it is, honey,
God's gonna take care of it." Though I never saw the
woman's face, her words still bring me comfort. Today,
reach out to someone. Be the hand of Christ.

Hebrews 2:14–18
Psalm 105:1–2, 3–4, 6–7, 8–9
Mark 1:29–39

# JANUARY 15

*"Oh, that today you would hear his voice."*
—HEBREWS 3:7

As a writer, my salary depends on the advances I receive
and the freelance projects that come my way. Though I
have consistent income from my day job, there are
definitely times when I need to stretch my funds. In the
lean months, I worry: *What if I can't make my house payment?*
*What if I get sick and I can't work?* Yet in the midst of these
loud, anxiety-filled questions, I hear the still, small voice of
God: "I will provide." Today, if you hear God's voice,
listen—and trust.

Hebrews 3:7–14
Psalm 95:6–7c, 8–9, 10–11
Mark 1:40–45

# JANUARY 16

*Unable to get near Jesus because of the crowd, they opened up the roof above him.*
—MARK 2:4

Four men took drastic action; they cut a hole in a roof. Why? Jesus was inside the house. And their friend, a man with paralysis, who was on a mat, needed to be healed. Sometimes we must take drastic action for our friends. When loved ones need the touch of Christ, we are called to cut a hole in heaven's roof, so to speak, to pray for them. Our intercessions become the mat on which we carry our friends to Christ.

Hebrews 4:1–5, 11
Psalm 78:3 and 4bc, 6c–7, 8
Mark 2:1–12

# JANUARY 17

• ST. ANTHONY, ABBOT •

*Let the words of my mouth . . . / find favor before you.*
—PSALM 19:15

Words hold great power. One small word of
encouragement can bring joy to a weary heart. But just a
few hurtful words can destroy a person's self-esteem and
well-being. Today, take care to speak kindly to others.
Share the encouraging words of Christ.

Hebrews 4:12–16
Psalm 19:8, 9, 10, 15
Mark 2:13–17

# JANUARY 18

*Do you not know that your body is a temple of the Holy Spirit within you?*
—1 CORINTHIANS 6:15

My friend Cindy stands about four feet, four inches. She is fifty-six years old and has lupus and leukemia. Her bones are brittle, and most of the time she is bent over. Often, she breaks a rib by turning in her bed. Though her body is broken, she spends her days reading the Scriptures and encouraging others. When I visit her, I am always greeted by the radiance of her smile. "Cindy, how do you remain so joyful?" I asked one day. She smiled and said, "The Holy Spirit lives within me."

1 Samuel 3:3b–10, 19
Psalm 40:2, 4, 7–8, 8–9, 10 (8a, 9a)
1 Corinthians 6:13c–15a, 17–20
John 1:35–42

# JANUARY 19

*He offered prayers and supplications with loud cries and tears.*
—HEBREWS 5:7

My Uncle Franny is the founder of Bridging, a thriving
outreach that provides household goods to poor residents
of Minneapolis. At eighty-six years of age, he's known for
telling heartwarming stories about the people he serves.
When he talks about people in need, he sometimes cries
dramatically. Once, when he was praying with a group of
businesspeople, he gathered everyone in a circle and asked
them to hold hands. "Lord, maybe someone in this group
can buy us a new truck," he prayed. Afterward, a CEO
wrote him out a check for ten thousand dollars. When we
pray fervently, with tears and loud cries, God hears our
requests—and sometimes, so do CEOs.

Hebrews 5:1–10
Psalm 110:1, 2, 3, 4
Mark 2:18

*God is not so unjust so as to overlook your work.*
—HEBREWS 6:10

My daughter Christina is in her mid-twenties. She works as the director of an outreach program that offers services to young adults with disabilities. Each month, she provides a calendar of events for her special clients: cooking classes, baseball games, trips to the lake. Though her salary is modest and the hours are long, she works tirelessly for those who are mentally challenged. "I hope I'm making a difference," she said to me one day. "You are doing God's work," I told her. If you are working hard for the kingdom of heaven, know that God notices.

Hebrews 6:10–20
Psalm 111:1–2, 4–5, 9 and 10c
Mark 2:23–28

# JANUARY 21

• ST. AGNES, VIRGIN AND MARTYR •

*Looking around at them with anger, and grieved at their hardness of heart, Jesus said to the man, "Stretch out your hand."*
—MARK 3:5

In today's Gospel, we learn what grieves the Lord. The story begins with the Pharisees watching Jesus in the synagogue. They want to see if he will defy Jewish law by healing a man on the Sabbath. They have no compassion for a man who is handicapped. And Jesus is grieved at their hardness of heart. While commandments provide a necessary framework for our faith, we must always be attuned to the voice of love.

Hebrews 7:1–3, 15–17
Psalm 110:1, 2, 3, 4
Mark 3:1–6

*Thursday*

# JANUARY 22

• ST. VINCENT, DEACON AND MARTYR •

*Jesus withdrew toward the sea with his disciples.*
—MARK 3:7

Above my fireplace hangs a canvas painting of the sea.
I bought it at a thrift store for twenty dollars, but it is one
of my greatest treasures. After a long day, I look at the
image and imagine the gently lapping waves and the soft
cries of seagulls. And I understand why Jesus often
withdrew to the sea. Maybe, as he walked the shoreline, he
found relaxation after a long day of ministering to the
people. Perhaps the waters brought calmness and
communion with his heavenly Father. At the end of this
day, withdraw to a place of calm, to be with God.

Hebrews 7:25–8:6
Psalm 40:7–8a, 8b–9, 10, 17
Mark 3:7–12

*"I will put my laws in their minds / and I will write them upon their hearts."*
—HEBREWS 8:10

The concept of moral conscience is beautifully described in article 6 of the *Catechism of the Catholic Church*: "For man has in his heart a law inscribed by God. His conscience is man's most secret core and his sanctuary. There, he is alone with God whose voice echoes in his depths." The next time you are struggling with a moral decision, visit the sanctuary of your conscience. Stay there for a while, alone with God. On the walls of your heart, God's law has been written. There in God's presence, you will know what to do.

Hebrews 8:6–13
Psalm 85:8 and 10, 11–12, 13–14
Mark 3:13–19

*Jesus came with his disciples into the house.*
—MARK 3:20

Recently, I sold the home in which my children grew up. After moving into a small cottage, I spent several weeks painting the walls, hanging curtains, and tending an overgrown garden. But one day, while organizing a closet, my eyes began to mist: *I miss our old house.* A few hours later, my sister Annie came over. "Let's invite Jesus to live here," she said. With that, she began praying over each room and claiming my new house for God. "Jesus, we welcome you to this cottage." Afterward, I felt an overwhelming sense of peace and joy. Have you invited Jesus into your house? If not, what can you do to welcome him?

Hebrews 9:2–3, 11–14
Psalm 47:2–3, 6–7, 8–9
Mark 3:20–21

*They too were in a boat mending their nets. Then he called them.*
—MARK 1:19

Sometimes, we hear the call of God when we are most comfortable with our lives. For instance, the disciples were in their boats, doing what they did most everyday—fishing. For them, life was predictable. Day after day, they tossed their nets into the sea, caught fish, and made a living. Then Jesus passed by. "Come follow me," he called out to them. In an instant, everything changed. Perhaps you have been blessed with a comfortable life. But never close your ears to the voice of Jesus. Sometimes, he wants to change everything.

Jonah 3:1–5, 10
Psalm 25:4–5, 6–7, 8–9 (4a)
1 Corinthians 7:29–31
Mark 1:14–20

*Monday*

# JANUARY 26

• SS. TIMOTHY AND TITUS, BISHOPS •

*"And if a house is divided against itself, that house will not be able to stand."*
—MARK 3:25

Every family has conflict. During the years I was raising my daughters, there were always little fights and disagreements. But we had a family rule: no one could go to bed angry. Throughout the years, that rule has served us well. Though my kids are now grown, we never let the sun go down without offering one another the gift of forgiveness. In today's Gospel, we are reminded that a house divided against itself cannot stand. Is your house divided? Try instating a new rule. Practice daily forgiveness. It's a great way to keep your home standing.

2 Timothy 1:1–8 or Titus 1:1–5
Psalm 96:1–2a, 2b–3, 7–8a, 10
Mark 3:22–30

*"For whoever does the will of God is my brother and sister and mother."*
—MARK 3:35

My mother just turned eighty-five. She's still quite sharp and lives in her own home. But many of her closest friends are passing away. She always seems to have a funeral or memorial service to attend. Yet in her neighborhood church, she has many friends, young and old, who love and care for her. "My church is like a family to me," Mom often says. Each of us will have to face the passing of loved ones. But Jesus provides a church family: faithful friends who will love us through our losses; mothers, brothers, and sisters in Christ.

Hebrews 10:1–10
Psalm 40:2 and 4ab, 7–8a, 10, 11
Mark 3:31–35

⇒ 59 ⇐

# JANUARY 28

• ST. THOMAS AQUINAS, PRIEST AND DOCTOR OF THE CHURCH •

*Some seed fell among thorns, and the thorns grew up and choked it.*
—MARK 4:7

When I first moved into my little cottage, I began pulling weeds from an overgrown garden. It was a daunting task. Tall thistles, most of them bearing thorns, were choking out the lilies and rosebushes. I had to wear gloves to protect my hands from the thorns. Now the flowers are thriving. They have sunlight and regular drinks of water from my hose. Jesus tells us that faith can be choked by "worldly anxiety and the lure of riches." What are the thistles in your faith life? Is it time for God to pull them out?

Hebrews 10:11–18
Psalm 110:1, 2, 3, 4
Mark 4:1–20

# JANUARY 29

*We must consider how to rouse one another to love and good works.*
—HEBREWS 10:24

When I was in college, there was a popular quote that was printed on posters, coffee mugs, and cards: "If you love somebody, let them go, for if they return, they were always yours. If they don't, they never were" (Khalil Gibran). Though the quote was overused, its message is worth pondering. Sometimes the best way to love someone is to refrain from clinging to him or her.

Hebrews 10:19–25
Psalm 24:1–2, 3–4ab, 5–6
Mark 4:21–25

*You need endurance to do the will of God.*
—HEBREWS 10:36

When I was in college, my two roommates were training
for a marathon. One day, they asked me to run eight miles
with them. "Sure," I said, even though I wasn't in shape.
About a mile into the run, I began to lag behind.
"Everything hurts," I told them. They refused to offer pity.
"You've got to build up your endurance." All these years
later, I work out regularly. I've learned that only consistent
exercise will keep my muscles strong. God wants us to
have spiritual endurance, too. So start training for the
marathon of faith that lies before you. Become strong
through prayer and sacrifice. Even when life hurts, keep
going. You need endurance to do the will of God.

Hebrews 10:32–39
Psalm 37:3–4, 5–6, 23–24, 39–40
Mark 4:26–34

# JANUARY 31

• ST. JOHN BOSCO, PRIEST •

*Jesus was in the stern, asleep on a cushion. They woke him and said to him, "Teacher, do you not care that we are perishing?"*
—MARK 4:38

Have you ever felt as if Jesus were sleeping? Perhaps you've been facing a raging storm of loss and uncertainty. Maybe you've heard yourself shout, "Lord, do you not care that I am perishing?" The disciples discovered that sometimes God is very quiet. But we mustn't be fooled by the silence. In the stillness of Christ's presence, the storms will calm.

Hebrews 11:1–2, 8–19
Luke 1:69–70, 71–72, 73–75
Mark 4:35–41

# FEBRUARY 1

*Brothers and sisters: I should like you to be free of anxieties.*
—1 CORINTHIANS 7:32

The dictionary definition of anxiety is this: "distress or uneasiness of mind caused by fear of danger or misfortune." Most of us experience these feelings at one time or another. Statistics show that more than forty million adults in the United States struggle with some sort of anxiety disorder or mental illness. I manage anxiety by working out regularly. My doctor says that physical exercise releases endorphins in the brain that are more powerful than morphine. Thus, every time I walk or jog, God gives me spiritual medication, treatment for my "uneasiness of mind." How do you manage your anxiety? Do you seek support from friends, family, and professionals? Can you accept such help as God's care for you?

Deuteronomy 18:15–20
Psalm 95:1–2, 6–7, 7–9 (8)
1 Corinthians 7:32–35
Mark 1:21–28

# FEBRUARY 2

• THE PRESENTATION OF THE LORD •

*"You yourself a sword will pierce—so that the thoughts of many hearts may be revealed."*
—LUKE 2:35

Michelangelo's sculpture the Pietà depicts Mary holding Jesus in her arms. Our Lord lies lifeless on her lap, his body bearing the wounds of crucifixion. There are nail marks on his hands and a scar where a spear pierced his side. Mary is wounded, too; her heart is gashed by grief. Those who have lost a loved one might find solace in this image. Mary understands, on a profound level, what true anguish feels like. In times of sorrow, she prays for us, as any loving mother would do. If you are grieving, reflect upon the image of the Pietà, and know that you are not alone.

Malachi 3:1–4
Psalm 24:7, 8, 9, 10 (10b)
Hebrews 2:14–18
Luke 2:22–40 or 2:22–32

# FEBRUARY 3

• ST. BLASE, BISHOP AND MARTYR • ST. ANSGAR, BISHOP •

*Jesus, aware at once that power had gone out from him, turned around
in the crowd and asked, "Who has touched my clothes?"*
—MARK 5:30

How does God receive and consider every prayer of every
day? We will never know. But in today's Gospel, we catch a
glimpse of God's efficiency. A great crowd has gathered
around Jesus. One resourceful woman, sick for many years,
decides to touch Jesus' clothing. Though throngs are
gathered around Jesus, somehow he feels her touch. And
with great compassion, he meets her need. We, too, can
reach out in our need, confident that God will feel
our touch.

Hebrews 12:1–4
Psalm 22:26b–27, 28 and 30, 31–32
Mark 5:21–43

# FEBRUARY 4

*At the time, all discipline seems a cause not for joy but for pain, yet later it brings the peaceful fruit of righteousness to those who are trained by it.*
—HEBREWS 12:11

Rachael, my youngest, was a spirited child. When she was about three years old, I took her grocery shopping with me. When I refused to buy her a package of sugary cookies, she threw a temper tantrum. She kicked and screamed, but I remained calm. "Rach, I'm sorry you are having such a bad day," I said. With that, I left the grocery cart in the store, and the two of us drove home. She never had a temper tantrum again. Sometimes God's discipline allows us to suffer the consequences of our actions. But God's patience makes it possible for us to learn and grow.

Hebrews 12:4–7, 11–15
Psalm 103:1–2, 13–14, 17–18a
Mark 6:1–6

*He instructed them to take nothing for the journey but a walking stick—no food, no sack, no money in their belts.*
—MARK 6:8

As the disciples set out on their journey, Jesus tells them to take nothing but a walking stick. No food? No money? No sack? Nope. Just a humble wooden stick to steady their steps. This might be puzzling to us. But think about it: the walking stick is a powerful metaphor. As believers, we can carry it at all times: it's whatever steadies our steps—a favorite prayer, Bible verse, poem, or song; a close friend or prayer partner. What helps you keep walking?

Hebrews 12:18–19, 21–24
Psalm 48:2–3ab, 3cd–4, 9, 10–11
Mark 6:7–13

*Do not neglect hospitality, for through it some have unknowingly
entertained angels.*
—HEBREWS 13:2

When I was in college, I often took the bus to a part-time
job at a newspaper downtown. One night, I worked until
ten o'clock. "Lord, keep me safe," I said, as I boarded the
bus. A kind-faced man sat down next to me. "I usually don't
take the bus at night," I told him. His eyes were filled with
fatherly concern. When the bus arrived at my college, he
asked, "Do you want me to walk you to your dorm?"
(I can't believe I trusted a stranger!) "Sure," I said. When we
arrived at my hall, I turned to thank him. But he was gone.
The Scriptures tell us that angels are at work in our world.
Have you ever entertained one?

Hebrews 13:1–8
Psalm 27:1, 3, 5, 8b–9abc
Mark 6:14–29

# FEBRUARY 7

*Beside restful waters he leads me; / he refreshes my soul.*
—PSALM 23:2

I've lived in Minnesota all my life. It's often called the Land of Ten Thousand Lakes. Within a two-mile radius of my home, there are streams, creeks, rivers, and lakes. I take advantage of this always-present water and think of it as an image of God's grace. We are always surrounded by it—really, we can't get away from it!

Hebrews 13:15–17, 20–21
Psalm 23:1–3a, 3b–4, 5, 6
Mark 6:30–34

# FEBRUARY 8

"*Let us go on to the nearby villages that I may preach there also. For this purpose have I come.*"
—MARK 1:38

Jesus knew his purpose: to bring God's love into the world. If you don't know what your purpose is, then look at the natural gifts and talents you have been given. I have a friend who is an amazing cook. Every Sunday, she makes a home-cooked meal and invites all those who are free to come. Another friend has the gift of hospitality. She makes homemade cards for folks who are sick, lonely, or grieving. Josh, a mentally disabled friend, smiles at everyone he meets. This Lent, figure out what your purpose is. Decide to use the gifts you've been given, your own way of bringing God's love to the world.

Job 7:1–4, 6–7
Psalm 147:1–2, 3–4, 5–6
1 Corinthians 9:16–19, 22–23
Mark 1:29–39

*God made the two great lights, the greater one to govern the day, and
the lesser one to govern the night.*
—GENESIS 1:16

My neighbor has a "moon light" in his backyard. Attached
to the top of a tall pole, the light is round and luminous, a
glowing globe that can easily be mistaken for the real
thing. The true moon, created by God, is a shining
reminder that we are loved. Tonight, dare to gaze at the
moon. Take in its beauty, and receive the love of
your Creator.

Genesis 1:1–19
Psalm 104:1–2a, 5–6, 10 and 12, 24 and 35c
Mark 6:53–56

*Then God said, "Let the earth bring forth all kinds of living creatures."*
—GENESIS 1:24

In Native American spirituality, everything in creation has a spirit and a name. This makes sense to me as I think about a chipmunk that lives underneath my porch. Each morning, he scurries past me as I make my way toward the driveway. Small and furry, he always stops to look me in the eye, as if he's saying, "Good morning! Have a good day!" I've named him Chip. I feel a strange kinship with him. We're both God's creatures, part of the same big family. Take time today to celebrate the small living creatures you meet on your path.

Genesis 1:20–2:4a
Psalm 8:4–5, 6–7, 8–9
Mark 7, 1–13

# FEBRUARY 11

• OUR LADY OF LOURDES •

*The LORD God formed man out of the clay of the ground and blew into
his nostrils the breath of life.*
—GENESIS 2:7

In Michelangelo's Sistine Chapel fresco *The Creation of
Adam*, God's hand reaches out to Adam, the first human.
Even though the hands of God and Adam are almost
touching, a small space separates them. Some have said
that the space is where God first infused Adam with life.
It's important to create spaces where God can breathe life
into our souls. For me, it's my sunlit dining room. Each
morning, I read the Scriptures at my table and make space
for God to be there, too, and to give me what is needed
for the day.

Genesis 2:4b–9, 15–17
Psalm 104:1–2a, 27–28, 29bc–3
Mark 7:14–23

# FEBRUARY 12

*He entered a house and wanted no one to know about it, but he could not escape notice.*
—MARK 7:24

The other evening, as I watched my niece's soccer game, I noticed an elderly woman rummaging through a garbage bin. Balancing herself with a walker, she plucked soda cans from the bin and placed them in a bag. I watched from the bleachers, not knowing how to respond. At the same time, a teenage boy walked past. He quickly finished his soft drink and called out, "Ma'am, would you like my can?" His kindness touched my heart. He was Christ to her. In today's Gospel, Jesus doesn't want attention, but it's hard to ignore love in action.

Genesis 2:18–25
Psalm 128:1–2, 3, 4–5
Mark 7:24–30

# FEBRUARY 13

*"Did God really tell you not to eat from any of the trees in the garden?"*
—GENESIS 3:1

One of the hardest decisions I've ever made was leaving
the security of my day job to write full-time for a year. It
was crazy, but I felt strongly that God was calling me to
give my undivided attention to a book project. During that
year, I often heard an inner voice say, "Did God really tell
you to do this?" I imagined a mini-devil with a pitchfork,
seeking my demise. But the Lord's voice (though just a
whisper) was stronger: *I am leading you* . . . In the end,
I wrote a book, and as a result, other projects followed. It's
not wise to second-guess decisions when you're
intentionally listening for God's guidance.

Genesis 3:1–8
Psalm 32:1–2, 5, 6, 7
Mark 7:31–37

*Saturday*

# FEBRUARY 14

• SS. CYRIL AND METHODIUS, BISHOPS •

*"Where can anyone get enough bread to satisfy them here in this deserted place?"*
—MARK 8:4

Are you waiting for Jesus to perform a miracle? He may need your help. Jesus fed four thousand people, but not without a few contributions from the crowd. Someone gave him bread. Another donated a few fish. Only after Jesus received these gifts did he bless and multiply them. During these Lenten weeks, we should pray for the impossible—but also ask, "Lord, what do you need from me?"

Genesis 3:9–24
Psalm 90:2, 3–4abc, 5–6, 12–13
Mark 8:1–10

# FEBRUARY 15

*Whether you eat or drink, or whatever you do, do everything for the glory of God.*
—1 CORINTHIANS 10:31

There's a famous photograph by Eric Enstrom simply titled *Grace*. It includes a small table, a loaf of bread, and some eyeglasses. An elderly peddler prays over the meager meal. His hands are folded, and his head is bowed. It's a powerful image that reminds us to be thankful for God's simple provisions. Whether feasting at a banquet or eating a meal alone, we can always say thanks.

Leviticus 13:1–2, 44–46
Psalm 32:1–2, 5, 11 (7)
1 Corinthians 10:31–11:1
Mark 1:40–4

# FEBRUARY 16

*The Pharisees came forward and began to argue with Jesus.*
—MARK 8:11

Have you ever had an angry exchange with God? I remember arguing with the Lord during my freshman year of college. That morning, the deposit was due on a trip I had planned to Israel. "Lord, I've prayed for months. Why haven't you provided this for me?" I said in a loud voice. I sounded like a spoiled child. Later that day, I received an unexpected check from a surprising source. It was enough to cover not only the deposit but also the entire trip. That day, I had started a loud argument with the Lord. But the Lord had quietly won.

Genesis 4:1–15, 25
Psalm 50:1 and 8, 16bc–17, 20–21
Mark 8:11–13

# FEBRUARY 17

• THE SEVEN HOLY FOUNDERS OF THE SERVITE ORDER •

*"Do you have eyes and not see, ears and not hear?"*
—MARK 8:18

Yesterday, I realized how important eye contact is. I was standing in line at the grocery store. The young woman at the cash register asked, "Do you want paper or plastic?" For a moment, our eyes met. I don't think I've ever seen so much despair in a person's eyes. I nodded to show I understood. Tears began to fill her eyes. "Thank you," she whispered. On this Lenten Tuesday, may God open our eyes, truly.

Genesis 6:5–8; 7:1–5, 10
Psalm 29:1a and 2, 3ac–4, 3b and 9c–10
Mark 8:14–21

# FEBRUARY 18

• ASH WEDNESDAY •

*Behold, now is the very acceptable time; behold, now is the day of salvation.*
—2 CORINTHIANS 6:2

That morning, my mother called and said, "It's a lovely day. Let's do something fun." I hesitated, busy writing devotions for this book. "Sure, Mom," I said. We spent the day shopping in a small town and riding an old-fashioned trolley. My younger sister bought us root-beer floats. Did I get any work done? None. But I now have a beautiful memory of my mother, laughing on the trolley. On this Ash Wednesday, consider how you are spending your time on this earth. Is this day the "very acceptable time" to give and receive love?

Joel 2:12–18
Psalm 51:3–4, 5–6ab, 12–13, 14 and 17
2 Corinthians 5:20–6:2
Matthew 6:1–6, 16–18

*Choose life, then, that you and your descendants may live, by loving the LORD, your God.*
—DEUTERONOMY 30:19

When I see a young mother with her handicapped child, I want to proclaim, "Blessed are you among women, and blessed is the fruit your womb." But I always restrain myself. Instead, I thank God that the woman has said yes to life, yes to faith, and yes to the untold blessings that come with sacrifice. How are you saying yes to life? In what ways are you caring for and protecting those who are poor and vulnerable? This Lent, if you have an opportunity to choose life, say yes.

Deuteronomy 30:15–20
Psalm 1:1–2, 3, 4 and 6
Luke 9:22–25

*Lift up your voice like a trumpet blast.*
—ISAIAH 58:1

As a teenager, I attended summer camp in Colorado. One morning, before the sun came up, a band of trumpet players stormed our cabin. The blast of their horns quickly roused everyone in our cabin from a deep sleep. Led by the band, we marched to the breakfast hall in our pajamas. What song did the trumpeters play? "When the Saints Go Marching In!" As members of Christ's body, the Church, we are saints, too. And sometimes we have the opportunity to sound the trumpet and proclaim the truth. And sometimes we're the ones who must hear the truth.

Isaiah 58:1–9a
Psalm 51:3–4, 5–6ab, 18–19
Matthew 9:14–15

*He will renew your strength, / and you shall be like a watered garden.*
—ISAIAH 58:11

Forty years ago, my father planted four oak trees in our front yard. Actually, they looked more like skinny sticks. Each day, my sisters and I took turns watering them. As we hosed the roots, my father made us wait until the water puddled into a circle. We often rolled our eyes. "Let the water run," Dad called to us from the porch. All these years later, the trees are tall pillars that decorate my childhood home. Deeply rooted, they are strong and stately. May we soak up God's strength and become just as rooted and lovely.

Isaiah 58:9b–14
Psalm 86:1–2, 3–4, 5–6
Luke 5:27–32

# FEBRUARY 22

• FIRST SUNDAY OF LENT •

*He was among wild beasts, and the angels ministered to him.*
—MARK 1:13

Imagine Jesus in the desert for forty days and nights. As he wandered through the blistering heat, he was exposed to dust and sandstorms. It's not a stretch to imagine him collapsing from exhaustion on the scorched land. Most likely, he felt pangs of loneliness. Yet in today's Gospel, Jesus shows us that the desert can be a place of spiritual enlightenment. He battled Satan and met wild beasts, but in the wasteland, beautiful angels ministered to his soul. Are you in the wilderness today? Wait for enlightenment—and angels.

Genesis 9:8–15
Psalm 25:4–5, 6–7, 8–9
1 Peter 3:18–22
Mark 1:12–15

# FEBRUARY 23

*"Lord, when did we see you hungry and feed you, or thirsty and give you drink?"*
—MATTHEW 25:37

Every now and then, I volunteer at a local center where thousands of meals are packed for those who need it. One morning, I worked with a young man who was mentally challenged. His job was to put stickers on the outside of plastic bags. He did his job meticulously, centering each sticker and smoothing it with his hand. As I watched, I imagined God smiling. This man was doing his part to offer food to the hungry.

Leviticus 19:1–2, 11–18
Psalm 19:8, 9, 10, 15
Matthew 25:31–46

# FEBRUARY 24

*Our Father who art in heaven.*
—MATTHEW 6:9

What comes to mind when you hear "Our Father"? Perhaps
you imagine a bearded grandfather enthroned in the
clouds. Maybe you envision an overbearing parent, ready
to punish your sins. If you had a father who was absent,
aloof, or abusive, the words might trigger hurtful
memories. In this season of grace and repentance, try
imagining God standing before you with outstretched
arms. Close your eyes and hear God say, "I love you. All is
forgiven. You are my child."

Isaiah 55:10–11
Psalm 34:4–5, 6–7, 16–17, 18–19
Matthew 6:7–15

# FEBRUARY 25

*A clean heart create for me, O God, / and a steadfast spirit renew within me.*
—PSALM 51:12

One of my favorite movies is *The Grinch Who Stole Christmas*. The mean-spirited Grinch goes through a conversion. After robbing the fictitious town of Whoville, the Grinch hears a surprising sound. Every Who is singing joyfully. At that moment, an X-ray machine is placed over the Grinch's heart; it has grown three times its size! Imagine such an X-ray of your own heart. What would you see? Bitterness? Gratitude? Anger? Joy?

Jonah 3:1–10
Psalm 51:3–4, 12–13, 18–19
Luke 11:29–32

# FEBRUARY 26

*Ask and it will be given to you; seek and you will find; knock and the door will be opened to you.*

—MATTHEW 7:7

When I was a young mother, my neighbor knocked on my door every afternoon. I dreaded her visits because she was a talker. It was hard to listen to her, especially when I had dinner to fix and three kids to care for. Sometimes I would pretend I didn't hear her persistent knocks. But I usually ended up welcoming her into my home. In today's Gospel, we are told to keep knocking when we need something from God. Unlike me in that neighbor situation, God welcomes our visit, whether every day or every hour.

Esther C:12, 14–16, 23–25
Psalm 138:1–2ab, 2cde–3, 7c–8
Matthew 7:7–12

# FEBRUARY 27

*"Go first and be reconciled with your brother."*
—MATTHEW 5:24

The other day, at the church where I work, I met Marie. As we got to know each other, she began telling me about her life. "Thirty-seven years ago, my husband and daughter were killed by a drunk driver. A year after they died, I forgave the young man who killed them." She talked about the power of forgiveness: "When I hugged the boy, God lifted a burden from my shoulders." I've been thinking about Marie for days. It's hard to forgive someone who doesn't deserve it. But Jesus calls us to take the initiative in matters of mercy: *Go first and be reconciled.*

Ezekiel 18:21–28
Psalm 130:1–2, 3–4, 5–7a, 7bc–8
Matthew 5:20–26

# FEBRUARY 28

*Blessed are they who observe his decrees, / who seek him with
all their heart.*
—PSALM 119:2

Whenever I struggle with an important decision, my
daughters will pat me on the back and say, "Mom, just
follow your heart." Their simple wisdom has served me
well. I've never regretted the guidance I've received from
my heart. It's the quiet voice of truth, God's prompting.
Are you facing a decision? Just follow your heart.

Deuteronomy 26:16–19
Psalm 119:1–2, 4–5, 7–8
Matthew 5:43–48

# MARCH 1

• SECOND SUNDAY OF LENT •

*And he was transfigured before them, and his clothes became dazzling white, such as no fuller on earth could bleach them.*
—MARK 9:2–3

Have you ever had an experience when God's presence dazzled you? Perhaps you received an unexpected provision or a startling answer to a prayer. Maybe a friend was cured of an illness. These miraculous moments always illuminate our faith. But what about those times when we walk in darkness and the light of Christ is veiled? In these difficult times, we must trust and believe that we are not alone. Even now, the light is shining, if beyond our sight.

Genesis 22:1–2, 9a, 10–13, 15–18
Psalm 116:10, 15, 16–17, 18–19 (116:9)
Romans 8:31b–34
Mark 9:2–10

*"Give and gifts will be given to you."*
—LUKE 6:38

That morning, I was the presenter at a retreat for young adults with disabilities. Has anyone ever seen God? I asked. A young man with cerebral palsy stood up: "I see God at church." A boy with Down syndrome pointed to the ceiling: "God is . . . in the stars . . . beeeeeeautiful!" One smiling man simply walked to the podium and patted me on the back. "You're doing a great job," he said. The answers kept coming from all corners of the room. Though I had come to tell these special people about God, they were telling me more. Try spending time with a person who appears to need your help and companionship. Go willing to give, but willing to learn, too.

Daniel 9:4b–10
Psalm 79:8, 9, 11 and 13
Luke 6:36–38

# MARCH 3

• ST. KATHARINE DREXEL, VIRGIN •

*Come now, let us set things right, says the LORD.*
—ISAIAH 1:18

Christina is my middle child. At twenty-five years of age, she has a wonderful way of combining compassion with humor. For example, last week the transmission on my car went out. As I sat at the kitchen table, lamenting the cost of repairs, Christina began pretending that she was a loving grandmother. She gently tapped my hand: "There, there, now. Everything will be OK." I can imagine God drawing near, saying, "Come now, let us set things right."

Isaiah 1:10, 16–20
Psalm 50:8–9, 16bc–17, 21 and 23
Matthew 23:1–12

*"Behold, we are going up to Jerusalem, and the Son of Man will be handed over to the chief priests and the scribes, and they will condemn him to death."*
—MATTHEW 20:18

In today's Gospel, we see Jesus anticipating his own death. We can assume he felt fear and anxiety about what was to come. But empowered by the love of his heavenly Father, he endured the cross and conquered death. For our sake, he accomplished what he was sent to do. Are you anticipating something difficult? Be not afraid. The power of God is with you.

Jeremiah 18:18–20
Psalm 31:5–6, 14, 15–16
Matthew 20:17–28

# MARCH 5

*And lying at the door was a poor man named Lazarus.*
—LUKE 16:20

Today's parable is sobering. A rich man is condemned because he ignores the needs of a poor man. How does this story speak to you? Does it make you want to volunteer at a homeless shelter or serve food at a soup kitchen? While these are wonderful ways to reach out, "the poor" are more present than you think. Perhaps a crabby coworker is hungry for your acceptance. Maybe a wayward child is starving for your attention. And every day we encounter people who need medical attention, extra money for emergencies, or simply better food on the table. May we walk through this Lenten season with our eyes—and hearts—open.

Jeremiah 17:5–10
Psalm 1:1–2, 3, 4 and 6
Luke 16:19–31

*When his brothers saw that their father loved him best of all his sons,*
*they hated him so much that they would not even greet him.*
—GENESIS 37:4

The country singer Lee Ann Womack has a song titled "I'll
Think of a Reason Later." In the lyrics, the artist describes
the jealousy she feels toward a woman who has stolen the
heart of her ex. The woman of her envy is beautiful and
also serves the poor. In the last part of the lyrics, Lee Ann
admits that while it's not Christian to judge a stranger, she
*really hates* this woman. It's a lighthearted song, but it has a
powerful message. Envy, if not dealt with, can destroy
relationships. Are you jealous of someone? Before it turns
to hatred, let God transform your heart.

Genesis 37:3–4, 12–13a, 17b–28a
Psalm 105:16–17, 18–19, 20–21
Matthew 21:33–43, 45–46

*He ran to his son, embraced him and kissed him.*
—LUKE 15:20

Can you relate to the prodigal son? Perhaps you've been living in a land of self-indulgence. Maybe your actions have ruined your finances or a few relationships. If you're wallowing in the mud somewhere, it's never too late to change. Simply go home to the mercy of God. Don't worry about condemnation from your Father. Your return will be celebrated with a welcoming embrace.

Micah 7:14–15, 18–20
Psalm 103:1–2, 3–4, 9–10, 11–12
Luke 15:1–3, 11–32

*But we proclaim Christ crucified.*
—1 CORINTHIANS 1:23

When I was a young girl, I went for a long walk with a friend. As we passed a park, we saw a teenage boy sitting at a picnic table. He looked up from his Bible and began witnessing to us about the love of Christ. He was nervous, and we could smell alcohol on his breath. Yet he was kind and sincere. All these years later, I still have a soft spot in my heart for that kid. At least he tried. Sometimes it's hard to share our faith. And yet today's reading beckons us to "proclaim Christ crucified." Today, try telling someone about Jesus. It's the effort that counts!

Exodus 20:1–17 or 20:1–3, 7–8, 12–17
Psalm 19:8, 9, 10, 11
1 Corinthians 1:22–25
John 2:13–25

*Monday*

# MARCH 9

• ST. FRANCES OF ROME, RELIGIOUS •

*As the hind longs for the running waters, / so my soul longs
for you, O God.*
—PSALM 42:2

One early summer morning as I pulled weeds from my
garden, I noticed two deer standing just feet away from
me, ears raised, and legs long and elegant. Every time I
moved to a different patch of weeds, they followed me
with graceful steps. I looked at them and they looked at
me. For about an hour, we shared the sacred silence of
morning. Sometimes when we commune with God, we
don't need to exchange words.

2 Kings 5:1–15b
Psalm 42:2, 3; 43:3, 4
Luke 4:24–30

*"Lord, if my brother sins against me, how often must I forgive him?"*
—MATTHEW 18:21

I waited in a drive-through line at the post office. Though it was Valentine's Day, I felt no love in that moment toward my mother. A day earlier we had argued. Now, I signed my name to a card I had bought out of obligation. *Why should I be the one to apologize?* Soon, the woman in front of me began honking at a man who was walking to the mailbox. When she realized that he was elderly, his hands brimming with valentines, she got out of her car and hugged him. "I'm sorry," she said. I watched as these two strangers illustrated the power of forgiveness. Now, I was just one car from the mailbox. I quickly reopened my mother's card and wrote, "I'm sorry—I love you, Mom."

Daniel 3:25, 34–43
Psalm 25:4–5ab, 6 and 7bc, 8–9
Matthew 18:21–35

*Wednesday*

# MARCH 11

*But teach them to your children and to your children's children.*
—DEUTERONOMY 4:9

About three months ago, I attended a fund-raiser directed by my twenty-five-year-old daughter Christina. Much to my amazement, she had organized everything: the food, a silent auction, and appearances by local celebrities. After she gave a speech, I pulled her aside. "Where did you learn how to do all this?" I asked. She laughed. "Mom, don't you remember when you were a director of faith formation? Every Sunday morning, you gave me jobs to do. I learned everything from you!" If you are raising or working with children, talk to them about your faith. Teach them the Scriptures and take them to Mass. They do in fact watch, listen, and learn.

Deuteronomy 4:1, 5–9
Psalm 147:12–13, 15–16, 19–20
Matthew 5:17–19

# MARCH 12

*Come, let us sing joyfully to the LORD.*
—PSALM 95:1

There's a Catholic church not far from my home. On Sunday mornings, familiar hymns chime from the bell tower above the church. Last Sunday morning, the bells began to play "Amazing Grace." As I walked to church, I began singing along with the bells: "'Tis Grace that brought me safe thus far and Grace will lead me home." The lyrics brought me comfort and peace. If you're struggling to pray, try singing some of the great hymns you know by heart.

Jeremiah 7:23–28
Psalm 95:1–2, 6–7, 8–9
Luke 11:14–23

*And no one dared to ask him any more questions.*
—MARK 12:34

As these Lenten days continue, try letting go of your
questions. Lean into the lessons you are learning. In all the
"unansweredness," blessings await.

Hosea 14:2–10
Psalm 81:6c–8a, 8bc–9, 10–11ab, 14 and 17
Mark 12:28–34

*Saturday*

# MARCH 14

*O God, be merciful to me a sinner.*
—LUKE 18:13

We all fall short of God's grace. Our thoughts deceive us.
We utter cruel words to loved ones. Each day, we commit
unkind deeds. On this Lenten Saturday, think about how
you respond to the sin in your life. Do you distance
yourself from God? Do you shame yourself with guilt? Do
you become depressed? Instead of beating yourself up, try
following the lead of the tax collector in today's Gospel.
Bow your head and pray, "O God, be merciful to me
a sinner."

Hosea 6:1–6
Psalm 51:3–4, 18–19, 20–21ab
Luke 18:9–14

*For by grace you have been saved through faith, and this is not from you; it is the gift of God; it is not from works, so no one may boast.*
—EPHESIANS 2:8–9

Will our good works get us into heaven? Is this even the right question? The way I see it, the God who paid the price for our sins deserves a big thank-you. Every time we reach out to those in need or console a hurting friend, we are offering our gratitude to God. We are modeling the love of Jesus. We are acknowledging the Christ who died, rose, and will come again. During this fourth week of Lent, reflect upon the grace that has saved you. Send an offering of thanks to God—a work of goodness and faith.

2 Chronicles 36:14–16, 19–23
Psalm 137:1–2, 3, 4–5, 6 (6ab)
Ephesians 2:4–10
John 3:14–21

# MARCH 16

*The things of the past shall not be remembered / or come to mind.*
—ISAIAH 65:17

When I sold the house my kids were raised in, I took one last walk through our home. Within these walls, three little girls had grown up. I remembered Christmas gatherings, good-night prayers, plays in the basement, prom pictures, soccer parties, rock music, and the smell of fingernail polish. I also remembered a marriage that ended and a daughter who died. I would take my precious remembrances with me. But grief, at least the worst of it, needed to stay behind. What "things of the past" do you need to leave behind?

Isaiah 65:17–21
Psalm 30:2 and 4, 5–6, 11–12a and 13b
John 4:43–54

# MARCH 17

• ST. PATRICK, BISHOP •

*"Do you want to be well?"*
—JOHN 5:6

As I struggled through a difficult time in my life, I started seeing a counselor once a week. "Do you want to feel better?" Ruth asked during our first meeting. "Of course," I responded. At the end of each session, Ruth would give me a few tasks to complete during the week. Months passed, but I never did my homework. One morning, Ruth got fed up with me. "When you are ready to make changes in your life, I'll be here to help. But we are done for today." And she walked out on me. From that day forward, I became serious about changing my life. Today, if you hear God ask, "Do you want to be well?" be careful how you answer. If you say yes, be prepared to do the homework.

Ezekiel 47:1–9, 12
Psalm 46:2–3, 5–6, 8–9
John 5:1–16

*I will never forget you.*
—ISAIAH 49:15

One spring day, when my daughter Christina was in first grade, her class was dismissed at noon. But when the school bus dropped her off, I wasn't there. I had circled the date on my calendar, but I was at the doctor's office with another daughter and simply forgot. When I arrived home at one o'clock, it was pouring rain. I saw Christina's backpack on the front porch and my heart sank. Minutes later, I found Christina safe and sound at my neighbor's home. That memory gives meaning to today's verse from Isaiah: "I will never forget you." I'm grateful that God is never preoccupied!

Isaiah 49:8–15
Psalm 145:8–9, 13cd–14, 17–18
John 5:17–30

*Thursday*

# MARCH 19

• ST. JOSEPH, SPOUSE OF THE BLESSED VIRGIN MARY •

*He believed, hoping against hope, that he would become "the father of many nations," according to what was said.*
—ROMANS 4:18

Whenever I drive past the local children's hospital, I see many windows. I know that behind those windows are very sick children and parents living through the most horrible moments of their lives. There is nothing harder than not being able to rescue a child from pain. Yet each day, in hospitals around the world, parents give up their right to protect their child from needles, monitors, chemo treatments, and IV machines. In the pain comes healing—and hope. Let us pray for those families today.

2 Samuel 7:4–5a, 12–14a, 16
Psalm 89:2–3, 4–5, 27 and 29
Romans 4:13, 16–18, 22
Matthew 1:16, 18–21, 24a or Luke 2:41–51a

*The LORD is close to the brokenhearted.*
—PSALM 34:19

There is actually a condition known as broken-heart syndrome, a temporary condition triggered by the death or loss of a loved one. The main symptom is sudden chest pain that mimics a heart attack. It's true that grief takes its toll on our physical and emotional health. Yet when we are attacked by heartache, our Great Physician is always available—even in the middle of the night, when the stab of sorrow seems most acute. Have you lost someone special? Remember that God specializes in broken hearts.

Wisdom 2:1a, 12–22
Psalm 34:17–18, 19–20, 21 and 23
John 7:1–2, 10, 25–30

*The guards answered: "Never before has anyone spoken like this man."*
—JOHN 7:46

Some years ago, a friend gave me an old King James Bible. She told me that it was a "red-letter edition." I was intrigued as she explained that the inspiration for the red printing for Jesus' words came from Luke 22:20: "This cup is the new testament in my blood, which I shed for you." While I'm quite fond of my Catholic Bible, during Lent I often open my red-letter Bible. The red words of Jesus remind me of his sacrifice on the cross. And I can understand why the guards in today's readings said, "Never before has anyone spoken like this man."

Jeremiah 11:18–20
Psalm 7:2–3, 9bc–10, 11–12
John 7:40–53

## Sunday

# MARCH 22

• FIFTH SUNDAY OF LENT •

*"I am troubled now. Yet, what should I say? 'Father, save me from this hour?' But it was for this purpose that I came to this hour."*
—JOHN 12:27

In today's Gospel, we see a troubled Jesus. He knows what is coming. He is about to suffer and die by crucifixion. Is he at peace with it? Not exactly. He's *troubled*. But he is also sure of God's calling on his life. When we pursue God's will, feeling troubled sometimes is part of the destiny. Following Jesus sometimes requires great sacrifice. But through prayer, our resolve will be firm. Like Jesus, we will know our purpose. And God will give us the strength to accomplish it.

Jeremiah 31:31–34
Psalm 51:3–4, 12–13, 14–15 (12a)
Hebrews 5:7–9
John 12:20–33

*"Let the one among you who is without sin be the first to throw a stone at her."*
—JOHN 8:7

In Victor Hugo's novel *Les Misérables*, Jean Valjean is imprisoned for nineteen years. His crime? He stole bread to feed his family. The story calls us to remember that things are not always as they seem. And in today's Gospel there may be more to the story. A woman is caught in the act of adultery. But maybe she was seduced or forced into the act. Perhaps her family abandoned her. Whatever the reason, Jesus forgives her "crime." He also calls those who condemn her to examine their own failings. There is nearly always more of the story we do not know.

Daniel 13:1–9, 15–17, 19–30, 33–62 or 13:41c–62
Psalm 23:1–3a, 3b–4, 5, 6
John 8:1–11

*Tuesday*

# MARCH 24

*In the day when I call, answer me speedily.*
—PSALM 102:2

Many of us have prayed for months or years for a specific prayer to be answered. But sometimes God will surprise us with a quick answer. I once prayed for the funds to pay my heating bill. That very day, an unexpected check arrived in the mail. And then there was my friend Roxanne. On the night before she had surgery for ovarian cancer, we prayed that God would heal her. The next day, the doctors were stunned. Her cancerous tumor had miraculously shrunk in size. Yet in the final analysis, it doesn't matter whether our prayers are answered slowly or speedily. What matters is that we pray.

Numbers 21:4–9
Psalm 102:2–3, 16–18, 19–21
John 8:21–30

*"Behold, you will conceive in your womb and bear a son, and you shall name him Jesus."*
—LUKE 1:31

When it comes to our relationship with God, is there any topic that is not discussable? In our readings for today, Mary is told that she will conceive a child by the power of the Holy Spirit. She responds by asking a question about a very private subject: sex. "How can this be, since I have no relations with a man?" she asks. Mary's candor should give us pause. There is nothing we can't discuss with God. In his loving presence, we can ask our toughest questions. We can share our private fears and failings. Our secrets are safe with him. Today, be candid in your prayers. It's the only way to be intimate with God.

Isaiah 7:10–14; 8:10
Psalm 40:7–8a, 8b–9, 10, 11 (8a, 9a)
Hebrews 10:4–10
Luke 1:26–38

# MARCH 26

*When Abram prostrated himself, God spoke to him.*
—GENESIS 17:3

In the Rite of Ordination, candidates for priesthood lie prostrate on the altar as a sign of total surrender to God. During the season of Lent, we surrender ourselves to God by praying, fasting, and giving alms. But perhaps you are being called to prostrate yourself before God in a different way. Is there someone you need to forgive, or someone to whom you need to confess a wrong? How about lying down on the altar of God's mercy for a few minutes. Leave your bitterness there. Then give attention to what God has shown you.

Genesis 17:3–9
Psalm 105:4–5, 6–7, 8–9
John 8:51–59

*But the LORD is with me, like a mighty champion.*
—JEREMIAH 20:11

There is a story about a group of young people who were
competing in a race. The activity was organized especially
for people with disabilities. As a man with Down syndrome
took the lead, he looked back at his competitors. One of
them had fallen on the track. Without hesitation, the man
came to a halt. Forfeiting his certain victory, he walked
back to the crying runner and helped him up. Together,
they ran hand in hand, toward the finish line. The story
sheds light on today's reading from the Psalms. Like that
man, our Lord is a mighty champion of love.

Jeremiah 20:10–13
Psalm 18:2–3a, 3bc–4, 5–6, 7
John 10:31–42

## Saturday
# MARCH 28

*I will turn their mourning into joy.*
—JEREMIAH 31:13

When a person begins to grieve a loss, it's hard to wake up in the morning. The awful realization that death has taken away a loved one is excruciating. But with God's help, the gashes of new grief can turn into sacred scars. At some point, a bereaved person might say, "I've survived." Though healing comes at a sluggish pace, it does come. If your Lenten mornings are filled with sorrow, just feel what needs to be felt. God is present in the pain. Rest assured that healing will come.

Ezekiel 37:21–28
Jeremiah 31:10, 11–12abcd, 13
John 11:45–56

*"You will find a colt tethered on which no one has ever sat."*
—MARK 11:2

Jesus rode a borrowed donkey into the Holy City. Though he was a king, his crown wasn't visible to the crowds who laid palms before him. There were no finely dressed soldiers to escort our Savior, just a band of tunic-clad disciples. The holy procession was not a display of power but a show of humility. During the upcoming week, this humility will be woven through every Gospel we hear. We will remember Jesus washing feet and breaking bread. We will recall his crown of thorns and the scourging he endured. We will see him stripped of his clothing and suffering on the cross for three agonizing hours. Let us begin this week the same way Jesus began the first Holy Week—with true humility.

PROCESSION:
Mark 11:1–10 or John 12:12–16

MASS:
Isaiah 50:4–7
Psalm 22:8–9, 17–18, 19–20, 23–24 (2a)
Philippians 2:6–11
Mark 14:1–15:47 or Mark 15:1–39

*Mary took a liter of costly perfumed oil.*
—JOHN 12:3

Mary anointed the feet of Jesus with costly perfume. It was an extravagant display of love. How do you display your love for others? The question brings to mind a Down syndrome man named Joe. A grocery bagger, Joe wanted to bring encouragement to his customers. With the help of his dad, he wrote a series of quotes, little day-brightening thoughts. He cut them out and took them to work. Each time he bagged someone's groceries, he would give that person a quote. Soon, people began lining up at Joe's counter. Even though other lanes were free, everyone wanted their daily inspiration from Joe. His encouragement became a priceless gift of love. Today, anoint the feet of Jesus. Share his love. God will bring about extravagant results.

Isaiah 42:1–7
Psalm 27:1, 2, 3, 13–14
John 12:1–11

*So he dipped the morsel and took it and handed it to Judas.*
—JOHN 13:26

I was purchasing a bag of chocolate coins. "Whatcha gonna do with these?" asked the teenage boy at the register. I explained that I worked at a church. "Tonight I'll be teaching about the betrayal of Jesus," I said. He smiled. "Oh yeah. Judas and the silver coins! Do you think Judas was sorry?" The question made me think. "I don't know."
While handing me my change, he said, "When I get to heaven I'm going to look around and see if Judas made it!" I drove home wondering about Judas's last moments. Before he hung himself, did he quietly repent? We'll never know, but the story has a moral. Up until our last breath, there is always time to repent.

Isaiah 49:1–6
Psalm 71:1–2, 3–4a, 5ab–6ab, 15 and 17
John 13:21–33, 36–38

*Wednesday*

# APRIL 1

• WEDNESDAY OF HOLY WEEK •

*My face I did not shield / from buffets and spitting.*
—ISAIAH 50:6

When Jesus was born, Mary and Joseph were the first to behold him. Like any new parents, they probably looked in awe at his face: the color of his eyes, the shape of his nose, and the soft blush of his cheeks. But thirty-three years later, the face they adored would be struck and spit upon. His forehead would bleed from a crown of thorns. On a cross, our tortured Savior would embody the prophecy of Isaiah: "so marred was his appearance, / beyond human semblance" (Isaiah 52:14). On this Holy Wednesday, imagine the face of the crucified Jesus. See his eyes gazing into yours. What do they communicate to you?

Isaiah 50:4–9a
Psalm 69:8–10, 21–22, 31 and 33–34
Matthew 26:14–25

# Thursday
# APRIL 2

• HOLY THURSDAY •

*Then he poured water into a basin and began to wash the disciples' feet.*
—JOHN 13:5

In downtown Minneapolis, there is a local outreach that serves thousands of homeless people: Sharing and Caring Hands. The founder of the outreach is an older mother named Mary Jo. Over the years, I have volunteered at the site. One morning, Mary Jo invited me to help her wash the feet of some of the clients. As I filled up basins with warm water, I wondered if it was ever hard for her to kneel before bare and battered feet. As I questioned her about this, she replied, "When I wash the feet of the poor, I am serving Christ. It's a powerful image." How are you called to kneel before Christ?

CHRISM MASS:
Isaiah 61:1–3a, 6a, 8b–9
Psalm 89:21–22, 25 and 27
Revelation 1:5–8
Luke 4:16–21

EVENING MASS OF THE
LORD'S SUPPER:
Exodus 12:1–8, 11–14
Psalm 116:12–13, 15–16bc, 17–18
1 Corinthians 11:23–26
John 13:1–15

*Friday*

# APRIL 3

• FRIDAY OF THE PASSION OF THE LORD (GOOD FRIDAY) •

*So Jesus came out, wearing the crown of thorns and purple cloak.*
—JOHN 19:5

Tradition has it that the crown of thorns was made from sharp thorns more than an inch long. When Jesus was struck in the head, the thorns must have caused excruciating pain. While it's difficult to imagine the torturous wreath, it provides us with a powerful image. When we are pierced with sorrow, Jesus knows how we feel. When our lives are pricked with loneliness and loss, he feels it deeply. On this Good Friday, be comforted. God wears and bears your pain.

Isaiah 52:13–53:12
Psalm 31:2, 6, 12–13, 15–16, 17, 25
Hebrews 4:14–16; 5:7–9
John 18:1–19:42

*"He has been raised; he is not here."*
—MARK 16:6

I don't visit my daughter's grave very often. It's not that I'm
avoiding my pain. I simply don't believe that she is there.
Before she passed away, the doctors diagnosed her with
pulmonary hypertension. She often had trouble catching
her breath. But now I relish the thought of her breathing
with ease. I like to imagine her dancing in heaven, smiling,
singing, twirling happily. She's not in her tomb. She's with
the resurrected God. The God who died and rose from the
dead. The God of hope and newness. The God who yearns
for every tomb to be empty.

VIGIL:

Genesis 1:1–2:2 or 1:1, 26–31a
Psalm 104:1–2, 5–6, 10, 12, 13–14, 24, 35 (30)
or 33:4–5, 6–7, 12–13, 20–22 (5b)
Genesis 22:1–18 or 22:1–2, 9a, 10–13, 15–18
Psalm 16:5, 8, 9–10, 11 (1)
Exodus 14:15–15:1
Exodus 15:1–2, 3–4, 5–6, 17–18 (1b)
Isaiah 54:5–14
Psalm 30:2, 4, 5–6, 11–12, 13 (2a)
Isaiah 55:1–11

Isaiah 12:2–3, 4, 5–6 (3)
Baruch 3:9–15, 3:32–4:4
Psalm 19:8, 9, 10, 11
Ezekiel 36:16–17a, 18–28
Psalm 42:3, 5; 43:3, 4 (42:2) or
Isaiah 12:2–3, 4bcd, 5–6 (3) or
Psalm 51:12–13, 14–15, 18–19 (12a)
Romans 6:3–11
Psalm 118:1–2, 16–17, 22–23
Mark 16:1–7

*Sunday*

# APRIL 5

*Think of what is above, not of what is on earth. For you have died,
and your life is hidden with Christ in God.*
—COLOSSIANS 3:1

When my daughter Rachael was a little girl, I helped her make a tent in our backyard. It was a makeshift refuge of old blankets slung over our clothesline. On warm summer days she would spend hours hidden away in her humble shelter. I'd often check on her as she played with dolls, listened to music, or read library books. "Are you OK?" I would ask. In a reprimanding tone, she would reply: "Don't worry, Mom. I'm safe!" I like to think of God as that kind of shelter. He is the risen Christ, the one who conquered death. In him, we are hidden, comfortable, and safe.

Acts 10:34a, 37–43
Psalm 118:1–2, 16–17, 22–23 (24)
Colossians 3:1–4 or 1 Corinthians 5:6b–8
John 20:1–9 or Mark 16:1–7; or (at afternoon or
evening Mass) Luke 24:13–35

*Therefore my heart is glad and my soul rejoices, / my body, too, abides in confidence; /*
*Because you will not abandon my soul to the nether world.*
—PSALM 16:9

Depression robs a person of joy. It steals away the feeling of peace and well-being. It also robs the body of energy.

How, then, should a person with depression interpret today's verse from the Psalms? First, remember that healing is possible. There are plenty of compassionate counselors who will become your companion on the road to recovery. Second, surround yourself with an unbreakable circle of support, trusted friends who will cheer you on. Most important, put your faith in the God of hope. He will never abandon your soul.

Acts 2:14, 22–33
Psalm 16:1–2a and 5, 7–8, 9–10, 11
Matthew 28:8–15

*Jesus said to her "Mary!" She turned and said to him in Hebrew,*
*"Rabbouni," which means Teacher.*
—JOHN 20:16

Mary Magdalene, upon recognizing the risen Christ, called him "Rabbouni." The word means "master" and "teacher." Throughout the Scriptures, there are many beautiful names and titles for God. One of my favorites is found in Isaiah 9:6: "Prince of Peace." I'm especially fond of this name because it reminds me of my identity as a believer. Like all believers, I am part of a royal family. One day, each of us will receive an eternal crown from our Prince of Peace. What is your favorite name for God? How does that name affect your identity?

Acts 2:36–41
Psalm 33:4–5, 18–19, 20 and 22
John 20:11–18

*But they urged him, "Stay with us, for it is nearly evening and the day is almost over."*
—LUKE 24:29

On the road to Emmaus, the disciples were preoccupied with grief. A few days earlier, their Lord had been crucified. As they walked in the darkness of their sorrow, they were unaware that the risen Christ was walking right beside them. Upon recognizing the Lord, they pleaded for him to stay with them. "It is nearly evening and the day is almost over," they told him. Are you walking in the shadows of grief? Try listening for the footsteps of Jesus. Even in the dark he is right beside you.

Acts 3:1–10
Psalm 105:1–2, 3–4, 6–7, 8–9
Luke 24:13–35

_Thursday_

# APRIL 9

_He stood in their midst and said to them, "Peace be with you."_
—LUKE 24:36

This past week, three people told me they were having a
bad day. A coworker complained that her water heater had
broken. My sister lamented the antics of her teenage son.
A friend spent hours in the emergency room for chest pain.
What has your day been like so far? If you are frustrated,
angry, or sad, imagine Jesus standing right next to you.
Receive the promise of his peace.

Acts 3:11–26
Psalm 8:2ab and 5, 6–7, 8–9
Luke 24:35–48

*Friday*

# APRIL 10

*Jesus said to them, "Come, have breakfast."*
—JOHN 21:12

Try to imagine today's Gospel. The morning sun is rising over Lake Tiberias. The risen Christ is standing over a charcoal fire, preparing breakfast for his friends. Gentle waves are lapping over the shore. The smell of roasting fish is wafting through the air, and there's bread to share. It's a humble meal, but it's celebratory. The worst is over.

The crucified Jesus is risen from the dead. Now that eternal life has been won, all Jesus wants to do is hang out with his friends. This story illustrates how deeply personal our relationship with Christ can be.

Acts 4:1–12
Psalm 118:1–2 and 4, 22–24, 25–27a
John 21:1–14

*Saturday*

# APRIL 11

*When they heard that he was alive and had been seen by her, they did not believe.*
—MARK 16:9

Last night, my youngest daughter, Rachael, called me on her cell phone. As we conversed, she mentioned that she was out for a walk. It was just starting to get dark, and I went into panic mode. What if she gets abducted? What if someone jumps out of a bush and rapes her? I didn't bother to pray for her protection. I was too busy worrying. Later that night (after I received an "I'm OK" text from Rachael) I began lamenting my lack of trust. I should've offered the simple prayer found in the Gospel of Mark: "Lord I believe; Help my unbelief" (Mark 9:24). When do you find it hard to trust in God? What makes it hard for you to believe?

Acts 4:13–21
Psalm 118:1 and 14–15ab, 16–18, 19–21
Mark 16:9–15

*Sunday*

# APRIL 12

• SECOND SUNDAY OF EASTER (OR SUNDAY OF DIVINE MERCY) •

*For the love of God is this, that we keep his commandments.*
—1 JOHN 5:3

I often go to garage sales with my eighty-five-year-old mother. We love finding designer clothes at bargain prices. Just the other day, as we walked toward a sale, a gentle rain began falling. "Mom, let me help you," I said. I extended my hand, but my mother whooshed her hand at me. "I'm fine!" But a few moments later, she reached out and grabbed my arm: "I'll hold on just this once." As the rain sprinkled on us, I smiled. She had taken care of me for decades. Now it was my turn. The Scriptures tell us to honor our father and mother. In doing so, we are given an opportunity to forgive the past or to return love.

Acts 4:32–35
Psalm 118:2–4, 13–15, 22–24 (1)
1 John 5:1–6
John 20:19–31

*The wind blows where it wills, and you can hear the sound it makes,*
*but you do not know where it comes from or where it goes.*
—JOHN 3:8

A few nights ago, a thunderstorm rumbled through our neighborhood, uprooting some of the sturdiest trees on the block. While picking up debris in the yard, I noticed that a large branch from the maple tree had fallen on the garage. Long before the storm, the branch had hung precariously from the tree, its leaves dead and brown for months. "Well, the wind took care of that!" I said. The Scriptures tell us that the Holy Spirit is like the wind, moving mightily in our lives, blowing away all that is dead and lifeless. If the Holy Spirit were to blow something away in your life, what would it be?

Acts 4:23–31
Psalm 2:1–3, 4–7a, 7b–9
John 3:1–8

*The community of believers was of one heart and mind.*
—ACTS 4:32

Before my father's funeral, I gathered with my mother and siblings (all ten of us) around my dad's casket. My brother Timmy began remembering how Dad orchestrated the "Sullivan Olympiad," a family event that took place every July in our backyard. Dad planned potato-sack races, lawn-dart tournaments, and a variety of relays. "Remember when Dad made us race around the block on our bikes?" Timmy said, chuckling. "He was blowing his whistle," my sister added. Each of us began sharing our own recollections of the Olympiad. By the time the funeral guests arrived, we were all doubled over with laughter. That day, we were bonded by memories and faith. Do you feel bonded to a family of believers? If not, where might you find one?

Acts 4:32–37
Psalm 93:1ab, 1cd–2, 5
John 3:7b–15

*Wednesday*

# APRIL 15

*Look to him that you may be radiant with joy.*
—PSALM 34:6

After my daughter Sarah was born with Down syndrome, I read many clinical reports. I quickly learned that my daughter had all the telltale signs of the condition: an extra chromosome, an upward slant to her eyes, and slow cognitive development. But the research didn't mention that Sarah's slanted eyes would shimmer with joy from the moment she was born until the day she died. The radiance of her smile and the purity of her heart were never referenced in a medical journal. Neither was the innate goodness that she shared with the world. When I think of true joy, the kind that comes from heaven, I will always think of Sarah. Who has brought true joy to your life?

Acts 5:17–26
Psalm 34:2–3, 4–5, 6–7, 8–9
John 3:16–21

*Thursday*

# APRIL 16

*He does not ration his gift of the Spirit.*
—JOHN 3:34

What does it mean to pray boldly? Perhaps it means trusting that God has no limits. Maybe it means believing that God will give you strength to face the impossibilities in your life. It may even mean surrendering your greatest fear. Are you in need of something big? Pray boldly. God does not ration the gift of the Spirit.

Acts 5:27–33
Psalm 34:2 and 9, 17–18, 19–20
John 3:31–36

# APRIL 17

*Jesus went up on the mountain, and there he sat down with his disciples.*
—JOHN 6:3

The faith journey has us climbing sometimes. We trudge along, uncertain. Maybe we become breathless. In moments of spiritual fatigue, we need to rest, if only for a moment. Though we may be in the middle of our climb, we must take time to sit down with Jesus. That's what the disciples did.

Acts 5:34–42
Psalm 27:1, 4, 13–14
John 6:1–15

*Give thanks to the LORD on the harp; / with the ten-stringed lyre
chant his praises.*
—PSALM 33:2

There's a little gift shop not far from my home. Sometimes,
when I'm having a stressful day, I stop there just to look at
the colorful trinkets that line the shelves. I especially love
the soothing harp music that plays throughout the store.
There's just something about a harp that makes me feel
closer to heaven. If you're feeling overwhelmed, treat
yourself to a CD of harp tunes. When you're stressed, play
the soul-centering music. Let the music turn your ears
to heaven.

Acts 6:1–7
Psalm 33:1–2, 4–5, 18–19
John 6:16–21

*The LORD will hear me when I call upon him.*
—PSALM 4:4

Now that I am an empty nester, I'm enjoying new freedoms. I now have an official office space where I can write. When my kids come over, they roll their eyes at all the healthy foods that fill my fridge. I'm spending more time exercising and cultivating friendships. But what's really changed is the way I pray. When I get up in the morning, I talk out loud to God. I praise him for the blessings he's bestowed on my life. I mention the names of loved ones. I ask him for the things I need. When I speak aloud to the Almighty, it feels as if he is right next to me. If you find yourself in a quiet place today, try talking out loud to God. He will enjoy the company.

Acts 3:13–15, 17–19
Psalm 4:2, 4, 7–8, 9 (7a)
1 John 2:1–5a
Luke 24:35–48

*Monday*

# APRIL 20

*"Do not work for food that perishes but for the food that endures for eternal life."*
—JOHN 6:27

Nutritionists tell us that our bodies need good food. To be energetic and strong, our daily diet should be balanced, with fruits, vegetables, dairy, and protein. But our spiritual diet is equally important. Our souls need an equal measure of prayer, fellowship, service, and rest. Unlike the food we eat each day, soul food will nourish us for eternity.

Acts 6:8–15
Psalm 119:23–24, 26–27, 29–30
John 6:22–29

# APRIL 21

• ST. ANSELM, BISHOP AND DOCTOR OF THE CHURCH •

*"Whoever comes to me will never hunger, and whoever believes in me will never thirst."*
—JOHN 6:35

When Thomas Aquinas was nearing fifty, he had written about a hundred works: commentaries, sermons, and treatises. But in the year 1273, he had a revelation that changed his life. Suddenly he stopped writing. Though a friend urged him to continue with his work, Thomas said: "I can write no more. I have seen things that make my writing like straw." He died a few months later. We don't know the details of his spiritual encounter. But after that experience, his hunger and thirst for God became all consuming, even to the point of giving up his greatest gift.

Acts 7:51–8:1a
Psalm 31:3cd–4, 6 and 7b and 8a, 17 and 21ab
John 6:30–35

⇒ 143 ⇐

*Wednesday*

# APRIL 22

*"For this is the will of my father, that everyone who sees the Son and believes in him may have eternal life, and I shall raise him on the last day."*
—JOHN 6:40

I once met a mother who had lost her thirty-year-old daughter to cancer: "I cannot believe in a God who allows such suffering." Having lost a child myself, I could relate to her spiritual crisis. Yet in the thunderous waves of grief, we must hold on to hope. For without hope, we cannot imagine heaven. Without hope, we cannot envision a joyous reunion with loved ones, and we will forfeit the promise of eternal life. Have you lost a loved one? Try asking God for one thing: hope.

Acts 8:1b–8
Psalm 66:1–3a, 4–5, 6–7a
John 6:35–40

*Thursday*

# APRIL 23

• ST. GEORGE, MARTYR • ST. ADALBERT, BISHOP AND MARTYR •

*"I am the bread of life."*
—JOHN 6:48

When I smell freshly baked bread, I'm immediately transported to my grandmother's home. On Sunday mornings when I was young, our family would gather in her sunlit kitchen. The aromas of fresh bread and cinnamon rolls would blend together, filling every corner of her house. Around her kitchen table, we would share mundane stories about our week. There was always plenty of laughter. As I recall those Sunday mornings, today's Gospel makes sense to me. Jesus is the bread of life. Like the aroma of my grandmother's bread, his presence fills every corner of our lives.

Acts 8:26–40
Psalm 66:8–9, 16–17, 20
John 6:44–51

*Immediately, things like scales fell from his eyes and he regained his sight.*
—ACTS 9:18

I have a close friend who stayed in an abusive relationship for more than twenty years. Though intelligent and self-aware, she spent decades making excuses for the violence of her partner. "I know he doesn't mean to hurt me," she used to say. When she finally found the courage to leave, she slowly began reengaging with life. She got a new job and moved into a small place she could afford. She began forging healthy friendships. She experienced a renewal of faith. Recently, I had coffee with her. "I'm proud of you," I told her. Her eyes brimmed with wisdom. "I will never 'unsee' the abuse again," she said. Are you "unseeing" something in your life? Maybe it's time to regain your sight.

Acts 9:1–20
Psalm 117:1bc, 2
John 6:52–59

*Saturday*

# APRIL 25

• ST. MARK, EVANGELIST •

*"The favors of the LORD I will sing forever."*
—PSALM 89:2

What will heaven be like? Surely we will know the
irrepressible joy of being re-united with loved ones. The
scriptures tell us that we will walk on streets of gold and
live in mansions. There will be luscious banquets and
gleaming crowns. We can also look forward to the singing
and dancing that will never end. What a glorious
celebration that will be.

1 Peter 5:5b–14
Psalm 89:2–3, 6–7, 16–17
Mark 16:15–20

*"I am the good shepherd. A good shepherd lays down his life
for the sheep."*
—JOHN 10:11

When I graduated from college, someone gave me a statue
of a shepherd holding a small lamb. Though I appreciated
the gift, the statue was quite ornate. So I put it in storage
and forgot about it for three decades. This past year when
I moved, I found the statue. I felt grateful for the ways in
which the Good Shepherd had guided me through the
years. Sometimes, when we look back on our lives, it's
easier to recognize how God has led us. At this point in
your life, do you know the Good Shepherd better than you
did in your youth?

Acts 4:8–12
Psalm 118:1, 8–9, 21–23, 26, 28, 29 (22)
1 John 3:1–2
John 10:11–18

*"I am the gate for the sheep."*
—JOHN 10:7

In our world, gates and walls are everywhere. There are gated communities that separate the wealthy from the poor. Along the border of Mexico, a wall prevents people from entering the United States. Even in relationships, we build gates of bitterness and lock them tightly. But Jesus tells us he is the "gate for the sheep." It's a gate of acceptance that is always unlocked. It is open to all: wealthy, poor, sinner, or saint.

Acts 11:1–18
Psalm 42:2–3; 43:3, 4
John 10:1–10

• ST. PETER CHANEL, PRIEST AND MARTYR • ST. LOUIS MARY DE MONTFORT, PRIEST •

*"How long are you going to keep us in suspense? If you are the Christ, tell us plainly."*
—JOHN 10:22

Have you ever felt that God was keeping you in suspense? Perhaps you are wondering if a relationship will work out or if a financial decision will prove to be favorable. Maybe you are anxious to hear the results of a medical test. In times of waiting, we usually won't hear from God in an audible voice. But he always clarifies his presence with a deep and indescribable peace. When we feel peace, God is speaking.

Acts 11:19–26
Psalm 87:1b–3, 4–5, 6–7
John 10:22–30

# *Wednesday*
# APRIL 29

*"I came into the world as light, so that everyone who believes in me*
*might not remain in darkness."*
—JOHN 12:46

Today I had lunch with Mary Beth, a long-time friend. She spoke of an argument she had with her teenage daughter. "We fought on the porch at midnight. It was so dark we couldn't see our faces," she told me. At one point, her daughter shouted, "Mom, do you love me?" In the shadows of night, a strange silence followed. Mary Beth opened her arms and hugged her child. "I love you more than my own life," she whispered. The darkness of their fight suddenly gave way to tenderness and truth.

Acts 12:24–13:5a
Psalm 67:2–3, 5, 6 and 8
John 12:44–50

*Thursday*

# APRIL 30

• ST. PIUS V, POPE AND RELIGIOUS •

*"My kindness is established forever."*
—PSALM 89:3

I recently saw a bumper sticker that read "Kindness Matters." I thought about how kindness has made a difference in my life. Here's the list I came up with: my mother's daily phone call, the neighbor who remembers to put out my garbage cans when I forget, an unexpected gift, a word of encouragement from my sister, an offer from a coworker to teach one of my classes, the stranger who gives me his parking space, the prayers of loved ones, supportive hugs. How has kindness made a difference in your life?

Acts 13:13–25
Psalm 89:2–3, 21–22, 25 and 27
John 13:16–20

*Friday*

# MAY 1

• ST. JOSEPH THE WORKER •

*And he did not work many deeds there because of their lack of faith.*
—MATTHEW 13:58

When we arrive in heaven, the Scriptures tell us that we will see God face-to-face (1 Corinthians 13:12). When I have my first conversation with God, I'll be curious to find out if my lack of faith prevented any miracles from happening. So often, my faith flounders. I'm good at praying for small blessings, but I often fail to pray for the stupendous. "God has better things to do than to perform personal miracles for me," I often say. But today's verse sounds more like a reprimand. God can't work mightily in our lives unless we let him. So start praying for the stupendous. You never know what might happen.

DAY:
Acts 13:26–33
Psalm 2:6–7, 8–9, 10–11ab
John 14:1–6

MEMORIAL:
Genesis 1:26–2:3 or
Colossians 3:13–15, 17, 23–24
Psalm 90:2, 3–4, 12–13, 14 and 16
Matthew 13:54–58

*Saturday*

# MAY 2

• ST. ATHANASIUS, BISHOP AND DOCTOR OF THE CHURCH •

*"The words I speak to you I do not speak on my own. The Father who
dwells within me is doing his works."*
—JOHN 14:10

Michelangelo painted the ceiling of the Sistine Chapel
between 1508 and 1512. His work is an overwhelming
masterpiece, a gift of art that illuminates nine scenes from
the book of Genesis. The great artist once said, "With few
words I shall make thee understand my soul." Centuries
later, his work still expresses the depth of what he could
not articulate: his spirituality. How does your work express
your spirituality?

Acts 13:44–52
Psalm 98:1, 2–3ab, 3cd–4
John 14:7–14

⋟ 154 ⋞

*For God is greater than our hearts and knows everything.*
—1 JOHN 3:20

The Our Father prayer conveys our deeply personal love of God. Our heavenly God is a compassionate provider, our protector from evil. He is full of mercy and compassion, the forgiver of every sin. He leads us toward his kingdom and delivers us from temptation. As we live in him, his will is done in us. The prayer is really a love story of sorts, a glimpse into the heart of God. If you have a quiet moment today, pray the Our Father slowly. As you meditate on each line, let the Holy Spirit explain who God is. Catch a glimpse of God's heart.

Acts 9:26–31
Psalm 22:26–27, 28, 30, 31–32 (26a)
1 John 3:18–24
John 15:1–8

## Monday

# MAY 4

*"Whoever loves me will be loved by my father, and I will love him and reveal myself to him."*
—JOHN 14:21

I attend a weekly Bible study group involving women of all ages, all of us seeking to grow in faith. Joyce, a woman in her mid-seventies was talking last week about her late husband. "He cherished me," she said. Joyce compared the love of her husband to the unfathomable love of our Lord. "How would we live our lives if we believed that we were cherished by God?" Joyce asked the group. The dictionary describes the word *cherish* in this way: "to hold dear: feel or show affection for." If you find yourself doubting God's love for you, just remember you are dear to him.

Acts 14:5–18
Psalm 115:1–2, 3–4, 15–16
John 14:21–26

*Your kingdom is a kingdom for all ages.*
—PSALM 145:13

My grandmother managed to pass along her faith without
the assistance of a computer or cell phone. She simply
served God in her daily life. In her basement sewing room,
she quietly hemmed clothes for family and friends. She
tended lovely flowers in her backyard. She cooked
homemade meals for us. She left prayer cards on her
kitchen table. She made pillows for her grandchildren. She
sent encouraging notes for no reason. She trusted the God
represented by the crucifixes in her home. She smiled.
Through watching her, I learned that living a life of faith
doesn't require a lot of electronics. Just love.

Acts 14:19–28
Psalm 145:10–11, 12–13ab, 21
John 14:27–31a

*Wednesday*

# MAY 6

*"Just as a branch cannot bear fruit on its own unless it remains on the vine, so neither can you unless you remain in me."*
—JOHN 15:4

A few days before I moved from my former home, I found something unexpected. While mowing the lawn, I noticed a blossom on a vine that was growing over my chimney. It was just one little bloom, an orange horn. In all the years that the vine had been growing, it had never had flowers. Now, the lone bloom seemed symbolic. After so many years of grief and loss, I was coming to life. Like the flower, I was experiencing the beauty of healing. Are you waiting for new life? Sometimes it takes a while. Your hope, if rooted in Christ, will one day bear fruit.

Acts 15:1–6
Psalm 122:1–2, 3–4ab, 4cd–5
John 15:1–8

*"And God, who knows the heart, bore witness by granting them the Holy Spirit just as he did us."*
—ACTS 15:8

About fifteen years ago, a young friend of mine committed suicide. For years afterward, her parents were in spiritual crisis. They wondered whether their deceased daughter received the punishment of hell. But a compassionate priest gave them wise counsel. "Yes, the church teaches that suicide is wrong, but as Christians, we are called to respond with compassion, not condemnation." He went on to tell the family that God knows the human heart. That counsel brought great healing to the family. We can pray compassionately for those who have died by suicide. We can trust that God knows each and every heart.

Acts 15:7–21
Psalm 96:1–2a, 2b–3, 10
John 15:9–11

*Friday*

# MAY 8

"No one has greater love than this, to lay down one's life for
one's friends."
—JOHN 15:13

Most of us remember where we were when terrorist attacks
of September 11, 2001, took down the World Trade
Center. I was glued to the television. Some of the most
unforgettable images were those of the firefighters who
were climbing the tower stairs to assist those who were
caught in the fire. Many responders never came back
down. They laid down their lives for total strangers. Their
sacrifice was an offering of true selflessness—and an
example for the rest of us.

Acts 15:22–31
Psalm 57:8–9, 10 and 12
John 15:12–17

*Saturday*

# MAY 9

*"If the world hates you, realize that it hated me first."*
—JOHN 15:18

On the news, we often see reports of "hate crimes," which refers to an injustice committed against a person because of his or her race, religion, ethnicity, sexual orientation, or disability. Jesus was a victim of a hate crime, targeted for his beliefs. He was killed because of who he was: king and Messiah. Unfortunately, we can expect to be "hated" for following Jesus. That's a little scary. Nobody wants to be hated for his or her beliefs. But we can take comfort in this. The God who was hated is in love with us.

Acts 16:1–10
Psalm 100:1b–2, 3, 5
John 15:18–21

*Sunday*

# MAY 10

• SIXTH SUNDAY OF EASTER •

*"As the Father loves me, so I also love you. Remain in my love."*
—JOHN 15:9

I had coffee with my daughter Christina a few weeks ago.
As we drank our lattes, she talked to me about her busy life
as a social worker. Her daily schedule was packed with
visits to clients. As she talked about graduate school, she
looked at me and paused. "You were a mom when you were
my age," she said. "I'd like to be a mom someday. Do you
think I'll be good at it?" I smiled. "Everything changed the
day you were born. I loved you immediately. I knew I
could give up everything for you." If it's hard to imagine
that God loves you, just think of him as a parent.

Acts 10:25–26, 34–35, 44–48
Psalm 98:1, 2–3, 3–4
1 John 4:7–10
John 15:9–17

⇉ 162 ⇇

*One of them, a woman named Lydia, a dealer in purple cloth, from the city of Thyatira, a worshiper of God, listened, and the Lord opened her heart to pay attention to what Paul was saying.*
—ACTS 16:14

Lydia was a businesswoman, a dealer in purple cloth. She had her own home and opened her door to Paul and his followers. When I imagine Lydia, I see a purple scarf draped around her head. Purple was the source of Lydia's identity, her livelihood. It's the color of the robe that Pontius Pilate gave Jesus before he died. It's the color of Jesus' love for you. Does the color purple give you an identity?

Acts 16:11–15
Psalm 149:1b–2, 3–4, 5–6a and 9b
John 15:26—16:4a

• SS. NEREUS AND ACHILLEUS, MARTYRS • ST. PANCRAS, MARTYR •

*"For if I do not go, the Advocate will not come to you."*
—JOHN 16:7

When someone is diagnosed with a disease such as cancer,
it's difficult for that person to think clearly. Many patients
in that situation now work with patient advocates, who
provide an important link between patients and doctors.
They offer hope. They clarify procedures and answer
questions. They help patients deal with their greatest fears
and frustrations. The Holy Spirit is our advocate, our link
to heaven. Under the Spirit's guidance, our relationship
with God is clarified. In times of fear or frustration, the
Spirit helps us find our way.

Acts 16:22–34
Psalm 138:1–2ab, 2cde–3, 7c–8
John 16:5–11

*Wednesday*

# MAY 13

• OUR LADY OF FATIMA •

*"Rather it is he who gives to everyone life and breath and everything."*
—ACTS 17:25

When we thank God for life and breath, it almost sounds
cliché. But the sacred rhythm of breathing can easily go
unnoticed. Every time we inhale, our diaphragm contracts
and our lungs expand. When we exhale, our diaphragm
relaxes. This pattern is nothing short of miraculous. Today,
pay attention to your breath. Let the fresh air sanctify your
body, mind, and soul. Celebrate the sacred rhythm of life.

Acts 17:15, 22–18:1
Psalm 148:1–2, 11–12, 13, 14
John 16:12–15

*Thursday*

# MAY 14

• ST. MATTHIAS, APOSTLE •

*I have called you friends, because I have told you everything I have heard from my Father.*
—JOHN 15:15

Matthias was chosen to replace Judas as apostle because Matthias had been with Jesus throughout his ministry. The apostles wanted someone who did not simply know about Jesus, but one who knew him. We can ask ourselves, "Do I know Jesus, as friend to friend?"

Acts 1:15–17, 20–26
Psalm 113:1–2, 3–4, 5–6, 7–8
John 15:9–17

*One night while Paul was in Corinth, the Lord said to him in a vision,*
*"Do not be afraid."*
—ACTS 18:9

I know someone who goes on a month-long retreat every July. She stays at a retreat center in northern Minnesota. In a one-room cabin, she is served a daily basket filled with bread and fruit. She uses the time to be quiet and to record her thoughts in a journal. While studying the Bible, she asks God for clarity in her life and prays for peace. "God always has something interesting to say," she once told me.

My friend's commitment to spend time with God is admirable. But most of us would find it hard to spend an entire month on retreat. Still, we can find pockets of quiet time each day. God has something interesting to say, no matter where we are or how much time we have.

Acts 18:9–18
Psalm 47:2–3, 4–5, 6–7
John 16:20–23

_Saturday_

# MAY 16

_He had been instructed in the Way of the Lord and, with ardent spirit,
spoke and taught accurately about Jesus._
—ACTS 18:25

While I was shopping for groceries last week, a young man handed me a coupon for a free tarot-card reading. He was clean cut, probably about fourteen years old. "My mom is really good at predicting the future," he said. I thought of telling him about my faith, but instead I said, "It's nice you are so proud of your mom!" As I drove home, I wondered if this boy had ever heard a Christian perspective on tarot cards or the occult. Had anyone ever taken the time to tell him about Jesus? I didn't know his past and could not predict his future, but I could pray for him and for the mom he was so proud of.

Acts 18:23–28
Psalm 47:2–3, 8–9, 10
John 16:23b–28

# MAY 17

• THE ASCENSION OF THE LORD •

*"For the LORD, the Most High, the awesome / is the great king over all the earth."*
—PSALM 47:3

What causes you to feel awe? When you see a lovely sunset or hold a newborn baby, do you feel a sense of wonder? Perhaps hearing a good homily or receiving a word of encouragement inspires your soul. Today, think about the presence of Christ in your life. How does he awe you?

Acts 1:1–11
Psalm 47:2–3, 6–7, 8–9 (6)
Ephesians 1:17–23 or 4:1–13 or 4:1–7, 11–13
Mark 16:15–20

*Monday*

# MAY 18

• ST. JOHN I, POPE AND MARTYR •

*Jesus answered them, "Do you believe now?"*
—JOHN 16:31

If you had documentation of all your prayers that have been answered during your lifetime, how long would your list be? Think of all the blessings you have received. Recall the joys you've known in relationships. Remember healings and financial provisions. Call to mind the sacred lessons you've learned in times of adversity. As you ponder the past, claim God's power over your present circumstances.

Acts 19:1–8
Psalm 68:2–3ab, 4–5acd, 6–7ab
John 16:29–33

*Tuesday*

# MAY 19

*I served the Lord with all humility and with the tears and trials that came to me.*
—ACTS 20:19

I went to Mass recently with my two daughters. During communion, the congregation began singing "On Eagles' Wings," by Michael Joncas. As I reached for the sunglasses in my purse, Rachael looked at me with anticipation. Then, she whispered to her sister, "Here we go again." My kids know that the song makes me cry. I can't help it. The lyrics bring to mind all the ways I've experienced grace in my life. I cry over the song because I'm overwhelmed with gratitude. Through every trial, we have been held in the palm of God's hand. Have you ever experienced cathartic tears? What stories did your tears call to mind?

Acts 20:17–27
Psalm 68:10–11, 20–21
John 17:1–11a

*They were all weeping loudly as they threw their arms around Paul and kissed him, for they were deeply distressed that he had said that they would never see his face again.*

—ACTS 20:38

Final good-byes are always heartbreaking. When we say farewell to a dying loved one, it's especially difficult to let go. But God tells us that our good-byes are temporary. In eternity, there will be a great reunion party. Jesus will greet us with open arms. Our loved ones, risen in Christ, will meet us with long embraces. All the good-byes of life will be replaced by happy hellos.

Acts 20:28–38
Psalm 68:29–30, 33–35a, 35bc–36ab
John 17:11b–19

# MAY 21

*The following night, the Lord stood by him and said, "Take courage."*
—ACTS 23:11

When I think of courage, I think of my longtime friends,
Marissa and Joel. Both of them are sidewalk counselors at a
Planned Parenthood clinic. Each month, they stand
outside the clinic and talk with young pregnant women. As
a couple, they share God's love and offer alternatives to
abortion: temporary housing, financial assistance, and
resources for medical care. Over the years, while helping
moms in need, Marissa and Joel have been threatened, spat
upon, and called names. Yet they continue to reach out to
these blessed women. Courage is a spiritual gift. Have you
recognized the courage God has given you?

Acts 22:30; 23:6–11
Psalm 16:1–2a and 5, 7–8, 9–10, 11
John 17:20–26

*Simon Peter answered him, "Yes, Lord, you know that I love you."*
—JOHN 21:15

When I was a little girl, I embroidered the word *Mom* on a white handkerchief. My novice stitching was crooked and snagged. Nonetheless, I gave the gift to my mom on her birthday. I couldn't figure out why she wouldn't stop crying. Years later, when my own daughters gave me handmade gifts, I did the same thing. I blubbered like a baby. "I love you so much!" I told them. God feels the same way about us. When we give him our lives, even the snagged and crooked parts, God sees our love.

Acts 25:13b–21
Psalm 103:1–2, 11–12, 19–20ab
John 21:15–19

*Saturday*

# MAY 23

*When Peter saw him, he said to Jesus, "Lord what about him?" Jesus said to him, "What if I want him to remain until I come? What concern is it of yours? You follow me."*
—JOHN 21:21–22

There's a stern tone to today's Scripture passage. Peter is wondering about the call of another disciple. In so many words, Jesus tells him, "Don't worry about him. Your job is to follow me!" It's easy to compare ourselves with fellow believers, especially those who are serving God in extraordinary ways. But God has given each of us a unique mission, one that only we can accomplish. Are you following your mission wholeheartedly? Or are you distracted by other disciples?

MORNING:
Acts 28:16–20, 30–31
Psalm 11:4, 5 and 7
John 21:20–22

# MAY 24

• PENTECOST SUNDAY •

*And suddenly there came from the sky a noise like a strong driving
wind, and it filled the entire house in which they were.*
—ACTS 2:2

On the weekends, my two daughters often stay with me.
Last Saturday afternoon, Christina decided to take a nap in
the front bedroom. It was a summer day, so she opened the
windows, turned on a fan, and quickly fell asleep. When I
passed by the room, the curtains were billowing and the
clothes in her closet were rustling. The fragrance of roses,
blooming outside her window, filled the room. As she
slept, the wind kept opening and shutting her door. The
Holy Spirit is like the summer air in Christina's room. Like
a restful breeze, the Spirit billows through our lives. A
rustling wind, the Spirit opens and shuts doors. The
fragrance of that presence is always near.

VIGIL:
Genesis 11:1–9 or Exodus 19:3–8a, 16–20b or
Ezekiel 37:1–14 or Joel 3:1–5
Psalm 104:1–2, 24, 35, 27–28, 29, 30
Romans 8:22–27
John 7:37–39

DAY:
Acts 2:1–11
Psalm 104:1, 24, 29–30, 31, 34
1 Corinthians 12:3b–7, 12–13 or
Galatians 5:16–25
John 20:19–23 or 15:26–27; 16:12–15

• ST. BEDE THE VENERABLE, PRIEST AND DOCTOR OF THE CHURCH •
ST. GREGORY VII, POPE • ST. MARY MAGDALENE DE' PAZZI, VIRGIN •

*"Go, sell what you have, and give to the poor and you will have*
*treasure in heaven."*
—MARK 10:21

Jesus invites a rich man to invest in eternity. But the
investment is too risky. The man simply cannot surrender
his possessions. The story today challenges each of us to
ask, *Are my things keeping me from serving the needy? Is my*
*flat-screen television preventing me from volunteering at the local food*
*pantry? Is my comfortable home isolating me from my neighbor in*
*need? Is my cell phone deafening my ears to the cry of the homeless,*
*the suffering, or the lonely?* In heaven, we will stand with those
we have served on the earth. Together, we will live in
mansions, eat at banquets, and dance on streets of gold.
May we prepare for eternity and invest our lives in service
to others.

Sirach 17:20–24
Psalm 32:1–2, 5, 6, 7
Mark 10:17–27

*"There is no one who has given up house or brothers or sisters or mother or father or children or lands for my sake and for the sake of the Gospel who will not receive a hundred times more now in this present age."*
—MARK 10:29

I have a friend who faithfully tithes 10 percent of her income. What's so amazing about her generosity is that she makes less than twenty thousand dollars a year. While her apartment is humble and her material possessions are few, she is one of the most joyful people I know. Folks from her parish often visit her. They bring her food, clothing, and gift cards. So many people are blessed by her presence. Are you having a difficult time giving God a percentage of your income? Don't focus on what you will lose. Begin by thanking God for the blessings that will come.

Sirach 35:1–12
Psalm 50:5–6, 7–8, 14 and 23
Mark 10:28–31

*Wednesday*

# MAY 27

*"For the Son of Man did not come to be served but to serve and to give his life as a ransom for many."*
—MARK 10:45

As a child, I heard stories about Uncle Bud. During the Great Depression, when my grandparents lost their farm, Bud was just a boy. During that time, he baled hay for other farmers and gave my grandmother his wages. "Mama, someday, I'll buy you a new farm," he told her. At nineteen years of age, my Uncle Bud died in World War II. After his death, the US government sent my grandparents a Purple Heart and ten thousand dollars, enough to build a home that three generations of family would enjoy. Like the sacrifice of Jesus, Bud's selflessness was a gift of love. Today, give thanks for someone who has sacrificed for your benefit.

Sirach 36:1, 4–5a, 10–17
Psalm 79:8, 9, 11 and 13
Mark 10:32–45

*Thursday*

# MAY 28

*By the word of the LORD the heavens were made.*
—PSALM 33:6

When I read a Scripture passage, I don't always understand what God is trying to say. Sometimes I must read a passage multiple times. Gradually, God's word comes alive in my thoughts. As I reflect upon the word, new insights and perspectives begin to surface. It's good to be patient when we ponder the sacred Scriptures. In the waiting, God speaks.

Sirach 42:15–25
Psalm 33:2–3, 4–5, 6–7, 8–9
Mark 10:46–52

*He overturned the tables of the money changers, and the seats of those who were selling doves.*
—MARK 11:15

Jesus got angry when his house was turned into a marketplace. His temple was not a store but a place of sanctification. This passage from Mark is a reminder that there are times when anger is appropriate. When someone is bullied or ridiculed, words of reprimand are in order. When we see a vulnerable person being taken advantage of, the injustice must be challenged. But while we are called to speak the truth, our impulses must be monitored carefully. When we experience anger, it's always good to ask, *Is my anger just? I am acting appropriately? Am I speaking for Christ?*

Sirach 44:1, 9–13
Psalm 149:1b–2, 3–4, 5–6a and 9b
Mark 11:11–26

*The law of the LORD is perfect, / refreshing the soul.*
—PSALM 19:8

I hardly ever drink coffee because the caffeine keeps me up at night. Instead, every morning I fill a mug with hot water and drop in a slice of lemon. As steam rises from my cup, I feel warm and comforted. The clean scent of lemon fills my senses. Unlike coffee, which gives me an immediate jolt, my morning drink brings calmness and peace. The law of the Lord is like that—refreshment to my soul.

Sirach 51:12cd–20
Psalm 19:8, 9, 10, 11
Mark 11:27–33

*"Did a people ever hear the voice of God speaking from the midst of fire,
as you did, and live?"*
—DEUTERONOMY 4:33

Everyone, at one time or another, experiences the fire of
adversity. When we pass through the flames of heartache
and loss, it's easy to think that God is absent. How can
God be present? Yet, from a burning bush, God spoke to
Moses. Do you remember what he said? *I have seen your
affliction . . .* When we walk through fire, we will not be
consumed. The Great I Am is with us.

Deuteronomy 4:32–34, 39–40
Psalm 33:4–5, 6, 9, 18–19, 20, 22 (12b)
Romans 8:14–17
Matthew 28:16–20

*"The stone that the builders rejected / has become the cornerstone."*
— MARK 12:10

Jesus experienced the pain of rejection. The religious leaders of his time wanted to do away with him. He was betrayed by Judas, one of the inner circle of disciples. The crowds that condemned him to death shouted, "Crucify him!" But Jesus persevered through rejection. He knew his identity. He was a heavenly king cloaked with skin. If you are experiencing rejection, remember that you are loved by a great king.

Tobit 1:3; 2:1a–8
Psalm 112:1b–2, 3b–4, 5–6
Mark 12:1–12

# JUNE 2

• SS. MARCELLINUS AND PETER, MARTYRS •

*"Repay to Caesar what belongs to Caesar and to God what belongs to God."*
—MARK 12:10

As a writer, I sign contracts to write books within a certain amount of time. With looming deadlines, I often feel pressure, especially when I sit before a blank computer screen. What if the words don't come? But whenever I feel panicky, I remember something very important. My words belong to God. Since I am just an instrument, I have a responsibility to share the gift I've been given. What is your gift? And what are you doing with it?

Tobit 2:9–14
Psalm 112:1–2, 7–8, 9
Mark 12:13–17

*Wednesday*

# JUNE 3

*Your ways, O LORD, make known to me, / teach me your paths.*
—PSALM 25:4

In Robert Frost's poem, "The Road Not Taken," the last
three lines read: "Two roads diverged in a wood, and I— /
I took the one less traveled by, / And that has made all the
difference." Life includes many forks in the road. And
sometimes the answer is not obvious, which is why we
need guidance: prayer, reflection, a word or a nudge
from God.

Tobit 3:1–11a, 16–17a
Psalm 25:2–3, 4–5ab, 6 and 7bc, 8–9
Mark 12:18–27

*Blessed are you who fear the LORD.*
—PSALM 128:1

When I was a young teacher, I worked at an all-girls Catholic school. One year, the girls' basketball team won the state championship. The next morning, Sister Phyllis, our principal, greeted the student body over the intercom system. "I just have one word to describe the performance of our team last night: *awesome!*" We may not always have words to describe what God is doing in and for us. But in these wordless moments, we might experience what the Scriptures call "the fear of the Lord." This is the knowledge, beyond a shadow of a doubt, that God is astonishing, magnificent, stupefying, glorious, and wondrous—and absolutely *awesome*.

Tobit 6:10–11; 7:1bcde, 9–17; 8:4–9a
Psalm 128:1–2, 3, 4–5
Mark 12:28–34

*Friday*

# JUNE 5

• ST. BONIFACE, BISHOP AND MARTYR •

*The LORD sets captives free.*
—PSALM 146:7

From time to time, we see people in handcuffs—on the news or on the street nearby. It's disturbing to see another human cuffed and chained. Yet many of us are bound by invisible shackles. When we insist on holding a grudge against someone, our bitterness tightens its grip. Entangled in our emotions and choices, we can't experience spiritual freedom. Are you free, truly? Or are you tangled? Such questions can lead to good prayer.

Tobit 11:5–17
Psalm 146:1b–2, 6c–7, 8–9a, 9bc–10
Mark 12:35–37

*"For they have all contributed from their surplus wealth, but she, from*
*her poverty, has contributed all she had, her whole livelihood."*
—MARK 12:44

I often rationalize that I can't possibly tithe 10 percent of
my income. I'm not a wealthy person. But then there's
today's Gospel. When I read it, I envision this poor women
giving all she had to God—"her whole livelihood." Ouch.
The passage prods me to examine my bank account. When
I review my finances, I'm amazed at how much money I
spend on frivolous purchases. There's definitely money in
my account to give to God's purposes in this world. I just
need to be more conscience of where it is.

Tobit 12:1, 5–15, 20
Tobit 13:2, 6efgh, 7, 8
Mark 12:38–44

*"Then he will show you a large upper room furnished and ready. Make the preparations for us there."*
—MARK 14:15

I am in the process of furnishing my new place. I'm shopping estate sales, and my sister is making curtains from beautiful fabric remnants. Yesterday my neighbor helped me cut down some overgrown trees in my backyard. Gradually, my house is turning into a space where I can pray, play, and share my life with loved ones. I think Jesus understands the importance of having a comfortable environment. He made arrangements for his disciples to eat the Passover dinner in a "large upper room furnished and ready." Today, take a good look at your living space. Is it homey? Is it a place where loved ones can gather comfortably? Is it furnished and ready for the Lord?

Exodus 24:3–8
Psalm 116:12–13, 15–16, 17–18 (13)
Hebrews 9:11–15
Mark 14:12–16, 22–26

*Blessed be the God and Father of our Lord Jesus Christ, the Father of
compassion and the God of all encouragement, who encourages us in
our every affliction, so that we may be able to encourage those who are
in any affliction.*
—2 CORINTHIANS 1:3–4

"Lord, make me wise," I prayed when I was younger.
I didn't know what I was asking. Now that I'm in my fifties,
I've discovered that wisdom is often gained in the hardest
moments of life. When we experience loss or death, we
master the art of "being present" to the bereaved. Adversity
teaches us lessons of empathy. Only when we walk
through darkness can we help guide others to light and
hope. It helps to remember that suffering offers the
opportunity for wisdom.

2 Corinthians 1:1–7
Psalm 34:2–3, 4–5, 6–7, 8–9
Matthew 5:1–12

*"You are the salt of the earth. But if salt loses its taste, with what can it be seasoned?"*
—MATTHEW 5:13

My mom often made hamburger goulash. One evening, she accidently added too much salt to the casserole. I still remember taking my first bite of the dish, along with my eight siblings. Faces crinkled and forks dropped. Finally, my brother Johnny said, "Mom, everything is fine but the taste." Jesus called us the salt of the earth. But we mustn't overdo our seasoning. If we share too many Bible verses, we might put off the people we hope to help. If we constantly preach and judge and try to fix things, others won't be able to stomach our presence for long. Most of the time, a little goes a long way. And our service to others is the best seasoning of all.

2 Corinthians 1:18–22
Psalm 119:129, 130, 131, 132, 133, 135
Matthew 5:13–16

*Not that of ourselves we are qualified to take credit for anything as coming from us; rather, our qualification comes from God.*
—2 CORINTHIANS 3:5

As a writer, I dread radio interviews for publicity. When I hear a program host introduce me to thousands of unknown listeners, I get a knot in my stomach. I'm insecure about not having an advanced degree. I graduated from college, but most of my writing colleagues are seasoned scholars who have attended schools of divinity and have studied theology. Their radio presentations are filled with eloquent teachings about faith. Nonetheless, I am qualified to share the Gospel. I'm a storyteller. It's a simple gift, but it equips me to share a humble message of grace. How has God qualified you to share the Good News?

2 Corinthians 3:4–11
Psalm 99:5, 6, 7, 8, 9
Matthew 5:17–19

*Thursday*

# JUNE 11

• ST. BARNABAS, APOSTLE •

*Then, completing their fasting and prayer, they laid hands on them and sent them off.*
—ACTS 13:3

If you were to raise someone from the dead, throngs of religious pilgrims might start gathering around your home. They might come in anticipation, hoping for their own miracles. They might light candles and sing hymns. But God has given each of us extraordinary healing powers. When we lay hands on a sick person, God touches her ailing spirit. When we comfort someone in pain, God raises him from the tomb of aloneness. When we forgive someone who doesn't deserve it, God cleanses the resentment from our lives. In today's Gospel, Jesus bestows healing powers on his disciples. The same power is within each of us.

Acts 11:21b–26; 13:1–3
Psalm 98:1, 2–3ab, 3cd–4, 5–6
Matthew 5:20–26

*To me, the very least of all the holy ones, this grace was given, to preach to the Gentiles the inscrutable riches of Christ.*
—EPHESIANS 3:8

All our skills and talents come from God. We can choose to develop our gifts, or we can spend our lives excusing ourselves. We can say, "I don't have time to be who I'm called to be." If you are not using your gifts, pray that God's grace will be poured out in your life. In time, he will show you where and how to use your gifts.

Hosea 11:1, 3–4, 8c–9
Isaiah 12:2–3, 4, 5–6 (3)
Ephesians 3:8–12, 14–19
John 19:31–37

# JUNE 13

• THE IMMACULATE HEART OF THE BLESSED VIRGIN MARY •

*Each year, his parents went to Jerusalem for the feast of Passover.*
—LUKE 2:41

Mary and Joseph were disciplined in their faith. Each year they honored the Passover by traveling to Jerusalem. In what ways do you honor God regularly? Do you participate in daily, weekly, or yearly disciplines that strengthen your faith?

2 Corinthians 5:14–21
Psalm 103:1–2,3–4,9–10,11–12
Luke 2:41–51

*Sunday*

# JUNE 14

• ELEVENTH SUNDAY IN ORDINARY TIME •

*Therefore, we aspire to please him.*
—2 CORINTHIANS 5:9

God is pleased by largeness of heart, not greatness of deed.
You can offer a small prayer while driving to work. You can
exchange a warm smile with a downcast stranger. You can
take the time to chat with your neighbor over the fence.
Today, please God by sharing small kindnesses.

Ezekiel 17:22–24
Psalm 92:2–3, 13–14, 15–16
2 Corinthians 5:6–10
Mark 4:26–34

⇒ 197 ⇐

# JUNE 15

*"If anyone wants to go to law with you over your tunic, hand him your cloak as well."*
—MATTHEW 5:40

I remember when our youth minister accepted a position at another parish. Before he left, I attended a going-away reception for him. At the gathering, several teens began sharing memories of him. One teenage boy recalled being injured in a soccer game and the youth minister taking off his shirt to use it as a bandage. "That one act of kindness changed me," said the teen. Each day we are given countless opportunities to go beyond what is expected. Our service to others makes a difference.

2 Corinthians 6:1–10
Psalm 98:1, 2b, 3ab, 3cd–4
Matthew 5:38–42

*I say this not by way of command, but to test the genuineness of your love.*
—2 CORINTHIANS 8:8

One day, after visiting the graves of loved ones, I decided to stroll around the cemetery. The sun was shining and I felt completely at peace. Soon, I passed a grassy area where several nuns were buried. There, etched on a simple stone, was the name of a Catholic nun I had known. She had been a seasoned instructor at the high school where I began my teaching career. As a young teacher, I often sought her counsel. Like a loving mother, she had guided me through the pitfalls of my first year of teaching. She had been my cheerleader, offering daily prayers for my success. Now, just seeing her name triggered great emotion in me. Her love, so pure and genuine, had changed my life. How has genuine love made a difference in your life?

2 Corinthians 8:1–9
Psalm 146:2, 5–6ab, 6c–7, 8–9a
Matthew 5:43–48

# JUNE 17

*So that in all things, always having all you need, you may have an
abundance for every good work.*
—2 CORINTHIANS 9:8

I have a friend who never prays for what she wants, only
for what she needs. I feel a little insecure around her
because I often ask God for small favors. Just today I
prayed that the weeds in my garden would stop taking
over my flowers. I also asked that my sister Annie would
come for a visit. I prayed for a new rug for my living room
too. I don't *need* any of these things. If I didn't receive them,
I wouldn't lose faith. But over the years, I've learned that
God provides for our daily needs but also delights in
giving us abundant gifts. Do you have everything you
need? Praise God! But remember, God grants unnecessary
favors too.

2 Corinthians 9:6–11
Psalm 112:1bc–2, 3–4, 9
Matthew 6:1–6, 16–18

# JUNE 18

But I am afraid that, as the serpent deceived Eve by his cunning, your
thoughts may be corrupted from a sincere and pure
commitment to Christ.
—2 CORINTHIANS 11:3

Our ruminations can remain a secret, if we so choose. But
God knows the musings of the heart and sees the anxiety
that taints mind and spirit. For instance, when we watch
violent or sexually explicit material, God grieves over our
hidden reflections. The good news is that God can purify
our thoughts. We just need to ask.

2 Corinthians 11:1–11
Psalm 111:1b–2, 3–4, 7–8
Matthew 6:7–15

*Friday*

# JUNE 19

• ST. ROMUALD, ABBOT •

*"Do not store up for yourselves treasure on earth, where moth and decay destroy, and thieves break in and steal."*
—MATTHEW 6:19

My adult daughters borrow my clothes. It's frustrating to go to my closet and discover that a blouse or scarf is missing. Several earrings have completely disappeared from my top drawer. About six months ago, I reprimanded them: "I need my stuff!" Later, I found myself wondering, *Are earrings really more important than a relationship with my daughters?* Eventually, we had a family meeting. We decided that all borrowed items must be returned within a week. So far, the girls have honored the new system. And I've learned that earrings shouldn't break up a family. The only treasure worth fighting for is love.

2 Corinthians 11:18, 21–30
Psalm 34:2–3, 4–5, 6–7
Matthew 6:19–23

# JUNE 20

*And I know that this man (whether in the body or out of the body I do not know, God knows) was caught up into Paradise and heard ineffable things, which no one may utter.*
—2 CORINTHIANS 12:3–4

Beethoven, one of the most influential composers in history, faced trials. In the early 1800s, his hearing began to deteriorate. During the last decade of his life, he was almost completely deaf. Yet Beethoven composed some of his greatest music in the soundless years of his life. Somewhere, in the quietness of his thoughts, he heard soul-stirring music. Perhaps God seems quiet in your life. Maybe adversity has muffled your faith. Listen patiently in the silence.

2 Corinthians 12:1–10
Psalm 34:8–9, 10–11, 12–13
Mark 6:24–34

# JUNE 21

*"Who then is this whom even wind and sea obey?"*
—MARK 4:41

Back in the early 1970s, my parents rented a houseboat. It was a luxury boat with five bedrooms and two bathrooms, more than enough room for our family of eleven. For a whole week, we floated along the tranquil Boundary Waters of Minnesota. Then, early one morning, a storm arose. Tall waves thrashed against the boat. Dishes fell from the cupboards. Mattresses were blown off our beds. I don't recall being afraid, though, because my father remained completely calm. As the lightning flashed, Dad steered our boat to a nearby island. From the shoreline, we watched the storm as if it were an exciting movie. If I could trust my dad to get us through the storm, can I trust God's guidance and protection through the expanse of my life?

Job 38:1, 8–11
Psalm 107:23–24, 25–26, 28–29, 30–31 (1b)
2 Corinthians 5:14–17
Mark 4:35–41

*Monday*

# JUNE 22

• ST. PAULINUS OF NOLA, BISHOP * ST. JOHN FISHER, BISHOP AND MARTYR *
ST. THOMAS MORE, MARTYR •

*"Stop judging, that you may not be judged. For as you judge, so will
you be judged."*
—MATTHEW 7:1

As I write this, many news stations are covering issues
related to same-sex marriage. It's an issue that divides
Christians of all denominations. But recently, Pope Francis
made headlines when he said, "Who am I to judge a gay
person?" His humble remark provides a wonderful example
for us to follow. It's not our job to judge another human
being. Unlike Jesus, we can't see into another person's
heart. Only God is privy to the complexities that dictate a
person's sexual orientation or preference. The Lord is far
more merciful than we can ever imagine.

Genesis 12:1–9
Psalm 33:12–13, 18–19, 20 and 22
Matthew 7:1–5

# JUNE 23

*"Do not give what is holy to dogs, or throw your pearls before swine."*
—MATTHEW 7:6

The Lord wants us to do what we can to heal broken relationships. But we must realize we can't do the "fixing." Sometimes we simply need to walk away from people who are perpetually abusive or unkind. We can't live true and holy lives if we are always on guard or fearful of what might happen next. Today, ask yourself, *Am I living as a treasured child of God? Or am I simply trying to survive?*

Genesis 13:2, 5–18
Psalm 15:2–3a, 3bc–4ab, 5
Matthew 7:6, 12–14

*Wednesday*

# JUNE 24

• THE NATIVITY OF ST. JOHN THE BAPTIST •

*To whomever I send you, you shall go.*
—JEREMIAH 1:7

If you sensed that God was calling you to a new job or
location, would you go? Or would it be easier to say, "I'm
comfortable with my current position. I like my
neighborhood. I have friends in my community."
Throughout the Scriptures, God calls his people to
"relocate." Think of Moses; of Mary and Joseph; of Peter,
the simple fisherman who left his job and eventually
became the first pope. When God calls us, we can always
say no. God gives us free will. But what if we say yes?

VIGIL:
Jeremiah 1:4–10
Psalm 71:1–2, 3–4a, 5–6ab, 15ab and 17
1 Peter 1:8–12
Luke 1:5–17

DAY:
Isaiah 49:1–6
Psalm 139:1b–3, 13–14ab, 14c–15
Acts 13:22–26
Luke 1:57–66, 80

*Not everyone who says to me, "Lord, Lord," will enter the Kingdom of heaven, but only the one who does the will of my Father.*
—MATTHEW 7:21

Seeking the will of God can be hard work, often requiring fervent prayer, complete submission, and an open heart. How do you know when you are seeking God? What emotions and desires motivate you? What gets in the way of your seeking?

Genesis 16:1–12, 15–16 or 16:6b–12, 15–16
Psalm 106:1b–2, 3–4a, 4b–5
Matthew 7:21–29

*"Can a child be born to a man who is a hundred years old? Or can
Sarah give birth at ninety?"*
—GENESIS 17:17

Abraham and Sarah were very old, but although they were
well past their childbearing years, God surprised them with
a child. If you are in the second half of life, be prepared for
the unexpected. I read a newspaper article about a
sixty-year-old woman who adopted a special needs child
with a terminal illness. "I'll love this child until he's ready
for heaven," she said. Even if you don't have the resources
for such extraordinary service, keep your heart open. God
is full of surprises!

Genesis 17:1, 9–10, 15–22
Psalm 128:1–2, 3, 4–5
Matthew 8:1–4

*"Lord, I am not worthy to have you enter under my roof; only say the
word and my servant will be healed."*
—MATTHEW 8:8

This morning while driving, I saw a red cardinal perched
on a white hydrangea. The sight was so beautiful that it
took my breath away. It was a perfect contrast of color,
life, and movement. The visual splendor was extraordinary,
and I felt unworthy to receive it. Driving onward, I
thought of God's artistic prowess. Such loveliness could
come only from God's hand. May we open our eyes today,
knowing that God has made us worthy and able to
receive beauty.

Genesis 18:1–15
Luke 1:46–47, 48–49, 50 and 53, 54–55
Matthew 8:5–17

# JUNE 28

*He took the child by the hand and said to her, "Talitha koum," which*
*means, "Little girl, I say to you, arise!"*
—MARK 5:41

A little girl has died. Jesus is at her bedside, along with the
girl's grieving parents. I've often envisioned that moment
when Jesus took the hand of that precious child.
Everything changed in that moment. Sickness and death
were gripped by God. The clasp of Christ brought healing.
Life was restored with a touch. If you've ever doubted
God's compassion, try imagining him holding your hand.
Feel the power of his touch. Allow him to change
everything.

Wisdom 1:13–15; 2:23–24
Psalm 30:2, 4, 5–6, 11, 12, 13 (2a)
2 Corinthians 8:7, 9, 13–15
Mark 5:21–43 or 5:21–24, 35b–43

*Monday*

# JUNE 29

• SS. PETER AND PAUL, APOSTLES •

*Then Peter took him by the right hand and raised him up, and*
*immediately his feet and ankles grew strong.*
—ACTS 3:7

Sometimes it's hard to get up in the morning. When we
have an illness or are experiencing a family struggle, it can
be difficult to face the day. But the act of getting up can be
very powerful. When we plant our feet on the ground and
stand upright, we are defying all the challenges we face.
We are saying, "God has raised me to another day of life.
In him, I am strong!" If you find it hard to get up, meditate
on today's Scripture passage. Imagine God making your
feet and ankles strong.

VIGIL:
Acts 3:1–10
Psalm 19:2–3, 4–5
Galatians 1:11–20
John 21:15–19

DAY:
Acts 12:1–11
Psalm 34:2–3, 4–5, 6–7, 8–9
2 Timothy 4:6–8, 17–18
Matthew 16:13–19

*Tuesday*

# JUNE 30

• THE FIRST HOLY MARTYRS OF THE HOLY ROMAN CHURCH •

*He got into a boat, [and] his disciples followed him.*
—MATTHEW 8:23

We never face life's storms alone. As the waves crash all around us, we can rest assured that we are in a very big boat and that God is at the helm. With great compassion, he will bring us to a new shore.

Genesis 19:15–29
Psalm 26:2–3, 9–10, 11–12
Matthew 8:23–27

⋛ 213 ⋜

## *Wednesday*

# JULY 1

• BLESSED JUNÍPERO SERRA, PRIEST •

*"Don't be afraid; God has heard the boy's cry in this plight of his."*
—GENESIS 21:17

I once heard a story about a little girl who lived on a farm in rural Minnesota. One day, the girl asked her father for a pony. The father, knowing it would be an expensive purchase, replied, "Why don't you pray about that?" The girl followed her father's suggestion. "Dear God, please give me a free pony." One afternoon, the two of them were driving along a rural road and they saw a sign that read "Free Pony." The father pulled over as an elderly man walked a small pony to their truck. "She's an older animal, just right for a little girl," the man said. Today, ask a child to pray for you. God delights in answering their prayers.

Genesis 21:5, 8–20a
Psalm 34:7–8, 10–11, 12–13
Matthew 8:28–34

*Jesus knew what they were thinking, and said, "Why do you harbor evil thoughts?"*
—MATTHEW 9:4

When we dislike another person, it's easy to harbor evil thoughts toward him or her. We can convince ourselves that the person doesn't deserve to be loved or valued. We can allow our dislike to devolve into active resentment or hatred. From time to time, if we are paying attention, we will hear Jesus say, "Why do you harbor evil thoughts?"

Genesis 22:1b–19
Psalm 115:1–2, 3–4, 5–6, 8–9
Matthew 9:1–8

*Then he said to Thomas, "Put your finger here and see my hands, and bring your hand and put it into my side, and do not be unbelieving, but believe." Thomas answered and said to him, " My Lord and my God!"*
—MATTHEW 9:9

Jesus invites Thomas to see the evidence, and believe. Jesus invites us to believe today. What will it take for us to follow the bidding of God?

Ephesians 2:19–22
Psalm 117:1bc, 2
John 20:24–29

*For the Lord has chosen Jacob for himself, / Israel for his own possession.*
—PSALM 135:4

It's easy to distance ourselves from the Lord when we think of ourselves as wretched sinners. "How can the Lord love me?" we might ask. But the Lord thinks of us as a treasured possession. Instead of focusing on your faults, try to imagine yourself as a priceless jewel in the hand of God. Let yourself gleam.

Genesis 27:1–5, 15–29
Psalm 135:1b–2, 3–4, 5–6
Matthew 9:14–17

*Three times I begged the Lord about this, that it might leave me, but he said to me, "My grace is sufficient for you."*
—2 CORINTHIANS 12:8

Perhaps you've experienced the disappointment of an unanswered prayer. I know I have. In times when God seems silent, we have a couple of choices. We can give up our faith, or we can embrace the mystery of God. The Scriptures tell us that God's ways are not our ways, and his thoughts are not our thoughts. Though the Lord can work miracles in our lives, he may, in his infinite wisdom, choose not to. But we can trust that God's love and grace will sustain us.

Ezekiel 2:2–5
Psalm 123:1–2, 2, 3–4 (2cd)
2 Corinthians 12:7–10
Mark 6:1–6

*Jacob then made this vow: "If God remains with me, to protect me on this journey I am making and to give me enough bread to eat and clothing to wear, and I come back safe to my father's house, the LORD shall be my God."*
—GENESIS 28:20

Today's passage is a beautiful one—but with a lot of "ifs." In so many words, Jacob is saying, "If I'm protected, if I have enough to eat, if I come back safely, *then* the Lord shall be my God." But what if Jacob had simply prayed, "If none of these things happen, I will still trust in the Lord"? Hidden in this verse is a challenge. If today you found yourself hungry, naked, or unprotected, would you still trust in God?

Genesis 28:10–22a
Psalm 91:1–2, 3–4, 14–15ab
Matthew 9:18–26

*But Jacob said, "I will not let you go until you bless me."*
—GENESIS 32:27

Have you ever fought for God's blessing? I know a mother who prayed for twenty years that her alcoholic son would find healing. While on her knees, she wrestled with the darkness in her son's life. She fought for his conversion as she prayed and read the Scriptures. She never loosened her grip on faith. Eventually, her prayers gave way to healing. Her son found his way to sobriety. If you are wrestling with darkness, don't give up the fight. Somewhere in the battle, a blessing awaits.

Genesis 32:23–33
Psalm 17:1b, 2–3, 6–7ab, 8b and 15
Matthew 9:32–38

*On the third day, Joseph said to his brothers: "Do this, and you shall live; for I am a God-fearing man."*
—GENESIS 42:18

What does a God-fearing man or woman look like? Does he shrink in terror before the Lord? Does she live in constant fear of God's power? Absolutely not! People who fear the Lord have a deep and personal friendship with Christ. They use their talents to build God's kingdom on earth. They laugh. They forgive. They pray. They trust that their sufferings are temporary, and they anticipate the joys of eternity. They forge close friendships, share their faith, and believe that they are God's beloved.

Genesis 41:55–57; 42:5–7a, 17–24a
Psalm 33:2–3, 10–11, 18–19
Matthew 10:1–7

*"As you enter a house, wish it peace."*
—MATTHEW 10:12

This morning, the man who picks up my trash did something unexpected. As his lumbering truck steered toward my driveway, I looked out my kitchen window. "Shoot!" I had forgotten to put my trash can by the curb. With haste, I slipped on my jacket and shoes. By the time I opened my front door, he had already rolled my can to his truck. After disposing of my trash, he returned the can to its place. Driving off, he waved. "Have a great day!" There are many ways to bless others, to extend peace.

Genesis 44:18–21, 23b–29; 45:1–5
Psalm 105:16–17, 18–19, 20–21
Matthew 10:7–15

*So be shrewd as serpents and simple as doves.*
—MATTHEW 10:16

Snakes are fearful creatures. They hiss and rattle. They have fangs, and some carry poisonous venom. But if you think about it, snakes are very vulnerable. They have no legs or ears, so they must slither on the ground. For the most part, they aren't large. But they have a keen instinct. If there's a threat, they can easily protect themselves. Jesus tells us that we must "be shrewd as serpents." Perhaps this means that we should trust the instincts God has given us.

Genesis 46:1–7, 28–30
Psalm 37:3–4, 18–19, 27–28, 39–40
Matthew 10:16–23

*And do not be afraid of those who kill the body but cannot kill the soul;*
*rather, be afraid of the one who can destroy both body and*
*soul in Gehenna.*
—MATTHEW 10:28

One of my favorite saints is Maximilian Kolbe. He was a
Franciscan friar of Polish descent. During World War II, he
was arrested for hiding Jewish people in his friary. While
imprisoned at the death camp of Auschwitz, he
volunteered to die in the place of a complete stranger, a
man who had a family. Kolbe sets the bar for sainthood
quite high. His story is a reminder that true faith asks a lot
of us. Sometimes it requires us to give up our lives, as
Jesus did.

Genesis 49:29–32; 50:15–26a
Psalm 105:1–2, 3–4, 6–7
Matthew 10:24–33

# JULY 12

*In him we were also chosen.*
—EPHESIANS 1:11

On summer evenings, when I was growing up, every kid in the neighborhood would gather in front of our house for a game of kickball. From the surrounding porches, parents would watch. My older sisters divided us into two teams. Usually my brothers would get picked first; they were fast runners. But eventually, every kid, from youngest to oldest, was chosen for a team. It didn't matter if you were a good player. Everyone got a chance to kick the ball. Sometimes, I ran around the bases while steering the stroller of my baby brother. God chooses each one of us. Though our abilities vary, we are drawn into the action to share our gifts—and our joy.

Amos 7:12–15
Psalm 85:9–10, 11–12, 13–14 (8)
Ephesians 1:3–14 or 1:3–10
Mark 6:7–13

*And whoever gives only a cup of cold water to one of these little ones to drink because he is a disciple—amen, I say to you, he will surely not lose his reward.*
—MATTHEW 10:42

On one of the hottest days of the summer, years ago, my little girls had a lemonade stand. While helping them set up a small table in our front yard, I overheard the three of them discussing how much to charge for each cup. After much deliberation, the oldest, Sarah, spoke up. "How 'bout free?" she said. With that, the kids made a sign that read "Free Lemonade." Within just a few hours, they had received "donations"—more than fifty dollars—from hot but grateful patrons. God's love is like a free cup of lemonade. When we receive it, we can't help but show our gratitude.

Exodus 1:8–14, 22
Psalm 124:1b–3, 4–6, 7–8
Matthew 10:34–11:1

*I have reached the watery depths; / the flood overwhelms me.*
—PSALM 69:3

One day I was biking along a trail near my home.
I stopped for a moment to rest on the bridge that
overlooked a small waterfall. On one side of the bridge the
current moved lazily, the quiet waters trickling over sand
and pebbles. But just underneath the bridge, the stream
began swirling over sharp stones. Just a few feet further,
the once-peaceful waters thrashed over a cliff and plunged
into a soft pool. The water was a mirror of my life. Though
I had swirled and crashed through many hardships, I had
always landed in a soft place: God's loving arms.

Exodus 2:1–15a
Psalm 69:3, 14, 30–31, 33–34
Matthew 11:20–24

*"For although you have hidden these things from the wise and the learned, you have revealed them to the childlike."*
—MATTHEW 11:25

God reveals himself to the childlike. When I think of what this means, I'm reminded of Cameron, a little girl from my parish. At three years of age, she is developmentally delayed. She is nonverbal, and she wears a hearing aid and thick pink glasses. After church yesterday, she handed me a note filled with scribbles. "She wrote it just for you," said Cameron's mother. Even though I couldn't read her "message," I was touched by her simple gift. We don't need to be "learned" to share God's message. All we need is a willingness to share love.

Exodus 3:1–6, 9–12
Psalm 103:1b–2, 3–4, 6–7
Matthew 11:25–27

*Thursday*

# JULY 16

• OUR LADY OF MOUNT CARMEL •

*"I am concerned about you."*
—EXODUS 3:16

"I am concerned about you"—today, hold those words in your heart. Imagine God speaking them to you. Remember that God sees what no one else sees. The sorrows you hide so well. The problems you cannot solve on your own. The anxieties that continue to rob you of joy. *I am concerned about you.* Let these words bring to mind the deeply personal love that God has for you.

Exodus 3:13–20
Psalm 105:1 and 5, 8–9, 24–25, 26–27
Matthew 11:28–30

*Friday*

# JULY 17

*Precious in the eyes of the LORD / is the death of his faithful ones.*
—PSALM 116:15

Every once in a while, I read the obituaries. For me, it's not a morbid practice. I'm always encouraged when I read about folks whose lives were defined by family, friendship, and faith. Obituaries call us to remember that life is temporary. When we read about well-lived lives, we are challenged to evaluate our own. In our daily routines, are we sharing faith and forgiveness? Are we using our gifts wisely? Do we love others the way God loves us? The next time you read the obituaries, be encouraged. Celebrate the gift of life and time and use both wisely.

Exodus 11:10–12:14
Psalm 116:12–13, 15 and 16bc, 17–18
Matthew 12:1–8

*They had rushed out of Egypt and had no opportunity even to prepare food for the journey.*
—EXODUS 12:39

There's a freeway not far from my home. It's framed with a tall wooden fence that serves as a sound barrier. Every morning, as I jog past the fence, I hear the sounds of cars, trucks, and buses racing past. Horns honk. Engines backfire. Wheels turn on concrete. Everyone is rushing to work. I must go to work, too. It's part of life.

But as I hear the sounds of rush hour, I close my eyes, remembering how important it is to carve out quiet time before the craziness begins. Though I am busy, just like the rest of the world, I need to begin my day in prayer. Prayer is sustenance, my food for the journey.

Exodus 12:37–42
Psalm 136:1 and 23–24, 10–12, 13–15
Matthew 12:14–21

# JULY 19

*"Come away by yourselves to a deserted place and rest a while."*
—MARK 6:30

It's good to have a deserted prayer space where we can rest
in the presence of Christ. But during our most demanding
moments, when we are surrounded by people and
overwhelmed by the duties of life, there are many creative
ways to rest in Christ. We can take a short walk on the
grounds of our workplace. If we are in a tense meeting or
facing an immediate decision, we can close our eyes and
ask for God's help. If we are driving from one destination
to another, we can turn off the radio and pray. No matter
how busy we are, we can retreat to the quietness of God's
heart, if only for a moment or two.

Jeremiah 23:1–6
Psalm 23:1–3, 3–4, 5, 6 (1)
Ephesians 2:13–18
Mark 6:30–34

*"Teacher, we wish to see a sign from you."*
—MATTHEW 12:38

Yesterday, I saw a sign from God at the post office. The line was long. As I waited for my turn to mail a package, a man pointed at my feet. He didn't speak English, but he was laughing. I looked down and saw that I was wearing two different sandals. I rolled my eyes and began giggling.

Soon everyone else in the line was laughing with us. "I once wore unmatched socks to work," one woman said.

A young teen added: "Last week my mom wore a garage-sale tag on her shirt." Even the postal workers were laughing. This unexpected joy filled the post office. I took it as a beautiful sign from God.

Exodus 14:5–18
Exodus 15:1bc–2, 3–4, 5–6
Matthew 12:38–42

*And he so clogged their chariot wheels that they could hardly drive.*
—EXODUS 14:25

When we are following the wrong path in life, it's as if we are driving a chariot through the Red Sea. While steering forward with our own plans, our wheels get clogged. The waves of failure cover us when we ignore the voice of God. In the slippery mud of stubbornness, we sink. On the other hand, when we are in God's will, the waters of his grace open before us. Are you moving effortlessly through an open sea? Or are the wheels of your chariot getting clogged?

Exodus 14:21–15:1
Exodus 15:8–9, 10 and 12, 17
Matthew 12:46–50

*Wednesday*

# JULY 22

• ST. MARY MAGDALENE •

*"This is the bread which the Lord has given you."*
—EXODUS 16:15

When we recite the Our Father, we pray these words: "Give us this day our daily bread." The prayer reminds us that God will give us everything we need for one day. We don't need to pack our freezer with a year's supply of food. We don't need to win the lottery to pay off the remainder of our mortgage. We don't need to store up material treasures for the future. While these provisions may give us the illusion of security, Jesus wants us to be secure in him.
What do you need from Jesus today?

Exodus 16:1–5, 9–15
Psalm 78:18–19, 23–24, 25–26, 27–28
John 20:1–2, 11–1

*Thursday*

# JULY 23

• ST. BRIDGET OF SWEDEN, RELIGIOUS •

*The disciples approached Jesus and said, "Why do you speak to the
crowd in parables?"*
—MATTHEW 13:10

Uncle Tony lived in my grandmother's basement. Growing
up, we heard stories about how wild Uncle Tony was in his
youth. He was an older man of few words, and his right ear
was crumpled. One Sunday morning, I was sitting with my
young siblings at our grandmother's kitchen table. "What
happened to Uncle Tony's ear?" My brother asked. "His ear
got run over by a horse and buggy." We started giggling.
Just then, we heard Uncle Tony's footsteps coming up the
stairs. "Yep, I got myself a cauliflower ear," he said. Years
later, the story of Uncle Tony's ear has been passed down
to three generations. Jesus told stories, too. His parables,
rooted in the everyday moments of life, were
unforgettable. Generations later, the family of God is still
sharing them.

Exodus 19:1–2, 9–11, 16–20b
Daniel 3:52, 53, 54, 55, 56
Matthew 13:10–17

# JULY 24

*The seed sown on rocky ground is the one who hears the word and receives it at once with joy. But he has no root and lasts only for a time.*
—MATTHEW 13:20–21

As a gardener, I often read articles about how to grow flowers and shrubs. I once read that trees should be planted in close proximity to one another. If trees grow together in groves, their roots begin to interlock. The reinforced root system can withstand strong winds and severe storms. That made me think of today's Gospel. As believers, we can't grow if we isolate ourselves. We need to interlock the roots of our faith with those of other believers. Bolstered by friendship and prayer, we can withstand any storm that comes.

Exodus 20:1–17
Psalm 19:8, 9, 10, 11
Matthew 13:18–23

*The LORD has done great things for us; / we are glad indeed.*
—PSALM 126:3

I always tell my kids, "You were the best thing that ever happened to me." I remember the moment they were born, and I still get the tingles. My children continue to be my greatest blessing. The love I have for them is just a tiny glimpse of God's love, I know. But I am grateful for the glimpse. Today, think about your life so far. What is the most wonderful blessing you have known? What great thing has God done for you?

2 Corinthians 4:7–15
Psalm 126:1bc–2ab, 2cd–3, 4–5, 6
Matthew 20:20–28

*"There is a boy here who has five barley loaves and two fish; but what good are these for so many?"*
—JOHN 6:9

On the journey of faith, we may be asked to sacrifice our financial security. We've all heard of folks who have given up great-paying jobs to serve in ministry. Then there are all those young parents who, for the sake of their kids, decide to live on one income. I remember when I gave up my day job to pursue my writing career. A wise friend gave me great counsel: "You're making less money but God will multiply what little you have." She was right. During that time, God's provisions came in miraculous ways. Today, allow God to multiply what little you have.

2 Kings 4:42–44
Psalm 145:10–11, 15–16, 17–18
Ephesians 4:1–6
John 6:1–15

*"The Kingdom of heaven is like a mustard seed that a person took and sowed in a field. It is the smallest of all the seeds, yet when full-grown it is the largest of plants."*
—MATTHEW 13:31–32

When we are young, we dream of the future: of finding true love, owning a home, securing the perfect job, or pursuing the gift that lies within us. Youthful dreams are like little seeds that God plants in our hearts. The trouble is, we all get older. The duties and responsibilities of life can overwhelm us. For many of us, our childhood dreams lie dormant for years. But little seeds are destined to grow into full-grown plants. Is it time for a dormant dream to come to life? Are you allowing God to bring it to fruition?

Exodus 32:15–24, 30–34
Psalm 106:19–20, 21–22, 23
Matthew 13:31–35

# JULY 28

*Merciful and gracious is the LORD, / slow to anger and abounding in kindness.*
—PSALM 103:8

I was arguing with my daughter as we drove through a snowstorm. I don't even remember what the fight was about. But as we raised our voices, our SUV began spinning on the ice. We ended up in a ditch. While waiting for help to come, we hugged each other, realizing how close we had come to death. "Anger got the best of us," I told my daughter. In today's Psalm, we read that the Lord is "slow to anger." The passage invites us to take a deep breath before we lash out at someone. Reactive anger can quickly get out of control. Angrily spoken words can easily turn into a great regret.

Exodus 33:7–11; 34:5b–9, 28
Psalm 103:6–7, 8–9, 10–11, 12–13
Matthew 13:36–43

*Martha, burdened with much serving, came to him and said, "Lord, do you not care that my sister has left me by myself to do the serving?"*
—LUKE 10:40

Tension is building between two sisters. Martha is working feverishly to prepare a meal for company. Mary is resting at the feet of Jesus. But what if Martha had followed Mary's lead? What if she had said, "I'll just sit with Jesus, too. We don't need really need to eat." Well, there wouldn't have been a delicious meal to enjoy. I suppose that would've been OK. But Martha's service was worthy of recognition. Remember, Jesus didn't reprimand her hard work. He simply chided her for being anxious about it. Is your daily work done with a happy heart? Or are you burdened with much "serving"?

Exodus 34:29–35
Psalm 99:5, 6, 7, 9
John 11:19–27 or Luke 10:38–42

*Thursday*

# JULY 30

• ST. PETER CHRYSOLOGUS, BISHOP AND DOCTOR OF THE CHURCH •

*"The Kingdom of heaven is like a net thrown into the sea, which collects fish of every kind."*
—MATTHEW 13:47

Two Jehovah's Witnesses knocked on my door yesterday. Both of them were well dressed, one a grandmotherly woman and the other a teenage girl. After taking several of their brochures, I told them, "I'm a Christian, but I admire your willingness to spread your message." They smiled. "We are Christians, too." As they went on their way, I said, "I'll pray for you." They promised to do the same. Today's Gospel reminds us that we are to cast our net into the sea of souls that surround us. What if we took that passage to heart? What if we had the zeal of the two women with the brochures? What if we began knocking on doors to spread the message of Christ?

Exodus 40:16–21, 34–38
Psalm 84:3, 4, 5–6a and 8a, 11
Matthew 13:47–53

*"Where did this man get such wisdom and mighty deeds?"*
—MATTHEW 13:54

The wrinkles on my grandmother's face were beautiful.
When "Mema" laughed, all the lines on her face curved
upward, like a hundred smiles. Now that I'm getting on in
years, I often think of Mema. Her wrinkles chronicled the
wisdom she had gained from life. In her younger years, she
lost the family farm, her home, my grandfather's income,
and her soldier son. But she never lost her faith. Though
life was hard, God made her strong on the inside. In her
older years, she was the wise matriarch of our family. She
was the most joyful person we knew. We should wear
wrinkles like smiles. We've earned them.

Leviticus 23:1, 4–11, 15–16, 27, 34b–37
Psalm 81:3–4, 5–6, 10–11ab
Matthew 13:54–58

# AUGUST 1

• ST. ALPHONSUS LIGUORI, BISHOP AND DOCTOR OF THE CHURCH •

*Now Herod had arrested John, bound him, and put him in prison.*
—MATTHEW 14:3

Today's Gospel is complicated. Herod was married to the wife of his half brother. When John the Baptist told Herod to repent, Herod threw him into prison. The illegal wife of Herod got involved, too, devising a plot to have John beheaded. The convoluted story reminds us that one sin can affect many people. How do you react when someone confronts you about sin? Do you minimize your actions or explain them away? Do you feel defensive or wrongly judged? Maybe you ridicule the call to repentance. Facing sin is never pleasant. But when we refuse to take responsibility for our actions, sometimes we can call on a John the Baptist to bring us to our senses.

Leviticus 25:1, 8–17
Psalm 67:2–3, 5, 7–8
Matthew 14:1–12

# AUGUST 2

*And be renewed in the spirit of your minds, and put on the new self,
created in God's way in righteousness and holiness of truth.*
—EPHESIANS 4:23–24

Are you going through a second-half-of-life crisis? Are you
bored? Do you long to do something different? Are you
questioning the decisions you made in your youth? If you
find yourself struggling with your identity, take a moment
to reflect upon today's verse from Ephesians. Maybe God is
in the process of creating a new you. In this season of life,
God may want to resurrect a dying relationship or open an
unexpected door. There might even be a risk that God
wants you to take. Today, surrender your old self to God
and make room for the new you.

Exodus 16:2–4, 12–15
Psalm 78:3–4, 23–24, 25, 54 (24b)
Ephesians 4:17, 20–24
John 6:24–35

*When Jesus heard of the death of John the Baptist, he withdrew in a
boat to a deserted place by himself.*
—MATTHEW 14:13

Grief is a lonely process. There are certain memories that
we can recall only in solitude. While it's comforting to cry
in the arms of another person, we must shed our most
sacred tears alone. Today's verse from Matthew speaks
volumes about the grief that Jesus felt after his friend John
passed away. He withdrew in a boat, to a deserted place by
himself. If you are grieving, allow yourself times of solitude
like Jesus did.

Numbers 11:4b–15
Psalm 81:12–13, 14–15, 16–17
Matthew 14:13–21

*When it was evening he was there alone.*
—MATTHEW 14:23

The homes of my past have always been filled with noise:
children's voices, footsteps, loud radios playing. But this is
a quieter season. I live alone in a small, peaceful space. My
kids visit often, friends come to dinner, and I'm close to my
neighbors. But late at night, when the house is still, I pray.
I welcome the silence. Sometimes I light candles and play
soft worship music. When you are alone, do you invite
God to join you?

Numbers 12:1–13
Psalm 51:3–4, 5–6ab, 6cd–7, 12–13
Matthew 14:22–36 or 15:1–2, 10–14

*"Have pity on me, Lord, Son of David! My daughter is tormented by a demon." But he did not say a word in answer to her.*
—MATTHEW 15:23

Have you ever felt that God wasn't listening? Mother Teresa did. In a diary written between the years 1959 and 1960, she wrote in the *Journal of Theological Reflection*, "In my soul, I feel just the terrible pain of loss, of God not wanting me." Yet Mother Teresa persevered in her vocation. Even though she experienced a crisis of faith, she continued to care for the desperate needs of others. Like Mother Teresa, and like the woman in this Gospel passage, we can keep calling on God's help, even when no help seems to be forthcoming.

Numbers 13:1–2, 25—14:1, 26–29a, 34–35
Psalm 106:6–7ab, 13–14, 21–22, 23
Matthew 15:21–28

*Thursday*

# AUGUST 6

• THE TRANSFIGURATION OF THE LORD •

*You will do well to be attentive to it, as to a lamp shining in a dark place, until day dawns and the morning star rises in your hearts.*
—2 PETER 1:19

When I moved into my new home, I turned a spare bedroom into a writing space. I bought an old desk and chair at a thrift shop and painted them white. I added a bookcase and a lamp with a crystal-trimmed shade. Sometimes, just before the sun rises, I wake up to write in my new space. In those shadowed moments, just before dawn, I search for inspiration. As I tap away at my computer, the crystals on the lamp shimmer. The soft light reminds me of Christ. Every person's sacred space is unique to that person. We can be attentive to Christ's light, however it comes to us.

Daniel 7:9–10, 13–14
Psalm 97:1–2, 5–6, 9
2 Peter 1:16–19
Mark 9:2–10

• ST. SIXTUS II, POPE, AND COMPANIONS, MARTYRS • ST. CAJETAN, PRIEST •

*"Did anything so great ever happen before? Was it ever heard of? Did a people ever hear the voice of God speaking from the midst of a fire as you did, and live?"*
—DEUTERONOMY 4:33

While standing before a burning bush, Moses was commissioned to lead God's people out of Egypt. Standing on hallowed ground, Moses felt comfortable enough to ask God questions. "I will be with you," God replied. We, too, can hear God's voice; we need only open the Scriptures. Those pages become our hallowed ground, and there we can ask questions, and our lives can be clarified.

Deuteronomy 4:32–40
Psalm 77:12–13, 14–15, 16 and 21
Matthew 16:24–28

# AUGUST 8

• ST. DOMINIC, PRIEST •

*Bind them at your wrist as a sign and let them be as a pendant*
*on your forehead.*
—DEUTERONOMY 6:8

For as long as I can remember, my father carried a photo in
his wallet, a picture of our family at a summer barbecue.
My mother still treasures the photo, though it's worn with
creases. In the Orthodox Jewish tradition, men bind little
black boxes (tefillin) to their arm and forehead. The boxes
contain parts of the Torah and serve to remind the wearer
that God's word must be kept in heart and mind at all
times. May we Christians carry God's word with us as
though we treasure it.

Deuteronomy 6:4–13
Psalm 18:2–3a, 3bc–4, 47 and 51
Matthew 17:14–20

⇒ 252 ⇐

*He prayed for death saying: "This is enough, O LORD!"*
—1 KINGS 19:4

Do you feel that you've had enough suffering? Today's
Scripture might bring comfort. The story begins with
Elijah praying for death. He's overwhelmed with what God
had asked of him. But an angel of the Lord brings him
"hearth cake" and water. It makes me think that God
wanted Elijah to feel especially cared for and loved. "Get
up and eat, else the journey will be too long for you!" the
angel tells Elijah (1 Kings 19:7). If you've endured great
suffering, eat the food that God has placed before you. Be
nourished by the care of family and friends. Receive
sustenance from a good counselor. Treat yourself to God's
grace. Otherwise, the journey may become too
long for you.

1 Kings 19:4–8
Psalm 34:2–3, 4–5, 6–7, 8–9 (9a)
Ephesians 4:30–5:2
John 6:41–51

*Blessed the man who fears the LORD.*
—PSALM 112:1

Every week, I go grocery shopping at our local supermarket. As I pass through the aisles with my cart, I rarely see anyone who is smiling. I've also noticed that very few people make eye contact with one another. Maybe it's just me, but sometimes I wonder if anyone in the store is happy. The Lord tells us that happiness comes from fearing him. This holy fear isn't about being frightened. It's about knowing that the glorious God of the universe loves us. The next time you go grocery shopping, bring the wondrous fear of the Lord with you. Make eye contact and smile at your fellow shoppers. Share the happiness of Christ.

2 Corinthians 9:6–10
Psalm 112:1–2, 5–6, 7–8, 9
John 12:24–26

*"See that you do not despise one of these little ones."*
—MATTHEW 18:10

Recently, a young mother told me about a Mass she attended with her children. During the first reading, her baby began to cry. An older woman turned around and gave her an unkind look. "We felt so unwelcome," the mom recalled. Jesus tells us not to despise the little ones. This weekend, if you see a young family in church, extend welcome, as Jesus did. Smile and make friendly eye contact. You may be distracted by the sound of their crying baby, but think of it as a holy interruption. Call to mind the sacredness of life, and praise God that you are witness to it.

Deuteronomy 31:1–8
Deuteronomy 32:3–4ab, 7, 8, 9 and 12
Matthew 18:1–5, 10, 12–14

# AUGUST 12

*"Whatever you loose on earth shall be loosed in heaven."*
—MATTHEW 18:18

Three years ago, a friend and I parted ways. We both hurled hurtful words, but neither of us asked the other for forgiveness. I have a hunch that God wants me to begin the process of reconciliation. But I'm scared. I don't want to open old wounds. What if this person rejects my offer of forgiveness? Or vice versa? Today's reading presents a challenge for me, and for everyone who struggles to forgive. Now, while we live and breathe on earth, we must free ourselves from bitterness and forgive those who have hurt us.

Deuteronomy 34:1–12
Psalm 66:1–3a, 5 and 8, 16–17
Matthew 18:15–20

*"Lord, if my brother sins against me, how often must I forgive him?"*
—MATTHEW 18:21

I've been friends with Maggie (name has been changed) for more than thirty years. In her teens, Maggie was a victim of clergy abuse. All these years later, she still has flashbacks of that betrayal. Her journey of forgiveness has been ongoing. When she has a panic attack during Mass, she manages it by closing her eyes and taking deep breaths. Then she prays, "Lord, I can't forgive, but you can." Today's reading reminds us that forgiveness demands much of us. The deeper we are hurt, the more mercy we must extend. If you are becoming weary with forgiving, try to close your eyes and pray: "Lord, I can't forgive, but you can."

Joshua 3:7–10a, 11, 13–17
Psalm 114:1–2, 3–4, 5–6
Matthew 18:21–19:1

*Give thanks to the LORD, for he is good.*
—PSALM 136:1

My sister Annie sent me a photo yesterday, a picture of a birthday cake that her husband had made for her. On the cake was a crown and a caption that read: "You are still my princess." I called her later and wished her a happy birthday. With a chuckle, I told her, "I want someone to call me a princess." Annie laughed. "I envy your life. I wish I could write. I wish I had a little house like yours." We agreed that God had given each of us good, if different, gifts. How do you feel about your life? How can you nurture gratitude and keep envy at bay?

Joshua 24:1–13
Psalm 136:1–3, 16–18, 21–22 and 24
Matthew 19:3–12

# AUGUST 15

• THE ASSUMPTION OF THE BLESSED VIRGIN MARY •

*A great sign appeared in the sky, a woman clothed with the sun, with the moon under her feet, and on her head a crown of twelve stars.*
—REVELATION 12:1

At the parish where I grew up, my grandmother had a special responsibility. She tended a garden that surrounded a statue of the Blessed Mother. The statue of Mary was made of white stone that sparkled in the sunlight. On top of Mary's head was a crown. Each spring, my grandmother polished the statue, pulled weeds, and planted petunias and marigolds. With great humility, she brought beauty to that sacred space. God gives each of us a garden to tend on earth. Where's your garden, and are you tending it?

VIGIL:
1 Chronicles 15:3–4, 15–16; 16:1–2
Psalm 132:6–7, 9–10, 13–14
1 Corinthians 15:54b–57
Luke 11:27–28

DAY:
Revelation 11:19a; 12:1–6a, 10ab
Psalm 45:10, 11, 12, 16
1 Corinthians 15:20–27
Luke 1:39–56

# AUGUST 16

*Watch carefully how you live, not as foolish persons but as wise,
making the most of the opportunity.*
—EPHESIANS 5:15

I have known people who deal with conflict by giving one
another the silent treatment, sometimes going weeks
without speaking. Each day of anger is another day of
resentment. When we hold on to bitterness, we miss
opportunities to forgive, to embrace each other, and to
begin again. Jesus tells us to watch carefully how we live.
Even in conflict, there are wonderful opportunities.

Proverbs 9:1–6
Psalm 34:2–3, 10–11, 12–13, 14–15 (9a)
Ephesians 5:15–20
John 6:51–58

# AUGUST 17

*And Jesus replied, "'You shall not kill.'"*
—MATTHEW 19:18

There are ways to kill our brother and sister that don't
require a physical weapon. Unkind words can kill
someone's spirit. When I was in college, an English
professor told me, "You aren't college material. You'll never
become a writer." I cried for days. Then another teacher, a
compassionate nun, saw my potential. In a sunlit convent
on campus, she taught me the craft of writing. "Keep at it,"
she would tell me. If I had believed the words of the
unkind professor, my hopes would have been dashed.
Today, share words of encouragement. Your words, spoken
in love, might change the trajectory of someone's life.

Judges 2:11–19
Psalm 106:34–35, 36–37, 39–40, 43ab and 44
Matthew 19:16–22

# AUGUST 18

*"But many who are first will be last, and the last will be first."*
—MATTHEW 19:30

This past Easter, a young mother took her handicapped son to the Easter mass at the Vatican. In an area designated for handicapped children, they waited for Pope Francis to arrive. When the Popemobile steered past them, an usher motioned for the driver to stop. The boy was held up. Pope Francis drew near and took the child into his arms and kissed him. The story is a beautiful reflection of God's love for us. Though we may feel as if we blend into a crowd, God notices us. While our disabilities may be many, the Lord wraps his arms around us. In God's embrace, we are blessed.

Judges 6:11–24a
Psalm 85:9, 11–12, 13–14
Matthew 19:23–30

*"Why do you stand here idle all day?" They answered, "Because no one has hired us."*
—MATTHEW 20:6–7

There's a place for idleness in the kingdom of God. While it's true that God has given each of us work to do, he is not an unreasonable boss. God did not create us to become workaholics. When we are driven by nonstop routines and schedules, we can easily become exhausted and crabby. How can we be an effective witness for Christ if we are always tired? Today, take a few mini-vacations. Give yourself permission to be unproductive, even if it's only for a few moments. Idleness can be rejuvenating.

Judges 9:6–15
Psalm 21:2–3, 4–5, 6–7
Matthew 20:1–16

*Thursday*

# AUGUST 20

• ST. BERNARD, ABBOT AND DOCTOR OF THE CHURCH •

*Some ignored the invitation and went away, one to his farm, another to his business.*
—MATTHEW 22:5

My kids grew up with Abbey. She's the daughter of one of my closest friends. Now in her twenties, Abbey is pregnant with her first child. Just the other day, I received an invitation to Abbey's baby shower. I have three other commitments on that day, but I wouldn't miss the shower. The event will be a celebration of shared memories and new life. It's no accident that Jesus used the analogy of a party invitation in this parable. I believe he was saying that his celebration of eternal life is something we won't want to miss.

Judges 11:29–39a
Psalm 40:5, 7–8a, 8b–9, 10
Matthew 22:1–14

*"You shall love the Lord, your God, with all your heart, with all your*
*soul, and with all your mind."*
—MATTHEW 22:37

Recently, a close friend gave me a ceramic heart adorned
with the words "There is no set path, just follow your
heart." As I hung the little trinket above my stove, I started
thinking about the human heart. It's that inner place within
each of us, that sacred space where faith, hope, and love
reside. No wonder God makes his home in the hearts of
believers. It's a beautiful place to live. If you are trying to
discern which life path to take, follow your heart. It will
lead you to beautiful things.

Ruth 1:1, 3–6, 14b–16, 22
Psalm 146:5–6ab, 6c–7, 8–9a, 9bc–10
Matthew 22:34–40

*Saturday*

# AUGUST 22

• THE QUEENSHIP OF THE BLESSED VIRGIN MARY •

*For they preach but they do not practice.*
—MATTHEW 23:3

There's a beautiful quote that is often attributed to St. Francis of Assisi: "Preach the Gospel, and if necessary, use words." We don't need to quote a Bible verse to share our faith. Each time we share a gift of kindness or mercy, we are giving testimony to the love of Christ.

Ruth 2:1–3, 8–11; 4:13–17
Psalm 128:1b–2, 3, 4, 5
Matthew 23:1–12

⇒266⇐

# AUGUST 23

• ST. ROSE OF LIMA •

*Since Jesus knew that his disciples were murmuring about this, he said to them, "Does this shock you?"*
—JOHN 6:61

A few months ago, I was shocked by a breathtaking rainbow that arced over my home. Looking upward, I stood with my hand over my mouth, awed by the sparkling prism of color. It was one of the most beautiful sights I have ever seen. For at least ten minutes, I took in the perfect display of shape, curve, and color. In the days to come, keep your eyes open for signs of God's presence. Look up. Look around. See God at work in your everyday life. Let yourself be awed.

Joshua 24:1–2a, 15–17, 18b
Psalm 34:2–3, 16–17, 18–19, 20–21 (9a)
Ephesians 5:21–32 or 5:2a, 25–32
John 6:60–69

*"Here is a true child of Israel. There is no duplicity in him."*
—JOHN 1:47

John Wooden was a famous American college basketball coach, a member of the Naismith Memorial Basketball Hall of Fame. He once said, "The true test of a man's character is what he does when no one is watching." In today's Scripture passage, we learn that true children of God are called to a high standard of character. We must live honestly, "without duplicity," even when no one is watching.

Revelation 21:9b–14
Psalm 145:10–11, 12–13, 17–18
John 1:45–51

*"Blind Pharisee, cleanse first the inside of the cup, so that the outside also may be clean."*
—MATTHEW 23:25

These days, there are many detox diets that promise to cleanse the body. Most of them suggest loading up on liquids that keep the kidneys, colon, and liver running smoothly. I have one friend who just started a cleansing diet. She's decided to drink nothing but "green" smoothies for a week. Yikes! While it's good to take care of our physical bodies, our spiritual health is equally important. What if we all went on a spiritual diet? What if we took the time to cleanse our spirit of bitterness and resentment? What if we detoxified ourselves of envy, dishonesty, and unresolved anger?

1 Thessalonians 2:1–8
Psalm 139:1–3, 4–6
Matthew 23:23–26

# AUGUST 26

*You recall brothers and sisters, our toil and drudgery. Working night
and day in order not to burden any of you.*
—1 THESSALONIANS 2:9

I usually stay in a hotel when I have a speaking
engagement. But every now and then, I'm invited to stay in
someone's home. I usually respond, "Thanks, but I don't
want to be a burden to anyone." I'm not sure why I'm so
quick to decline an offer of hospitality. When I allow
myself to be "taken care of," I'm giving someone an
opportunity to serve. I'm working on becoming better at
receiving gifts from others. The next time I'm invited to
stay in someone's home, I'm going to say yes. Jesus often
stayed in the homes of his followers, and his example is a
good one to follow.

1 Thessalonians 2:9–13
Psalm 139:7–8, 9–10, 11–12ab
Matthew 23:27–32

*Jesus said to his disciples: "Stay awake!"*
—MATTHEW 24:42

In Minnesota, it's hard to get up on winter mornings.
Usually it stays dark until about seven thirty. Outside my
window, the winds howl. As I huddle under mounds of
blankets, I want to sleep. But my workday awaits. *Wake up!*
I tell myself. Likewise, it's sometimes hard to rouse
ourselves for the work of Christ. Serving others demands
that we leave our warm and comfortable life. When we
encourage the bereaved, we must wake up to their pain. In
sharing compassion, we must open our eyes to those who
are suffering. But the work of the kingdom awaits. And
Jesus will help us wake up and get started.

1 Thessalonians 3:7–13
Psalm 90:3–5a, 12–13, 14 and 17
Matthew 24:42–51

*Friday*

# AUGUST 28

• ST. AUGUSTINE, BISHOP AND DOCTOR OF THE CHURCH •

*The foolish ones, when taking their lamps, brought no oil with them,*
*but the wise brought flasks of oil with their lamps.*
—MATTHEW 25:3

A couple of years ago, I made popcorn the old-fashioned
way, on the stove. After I poured oil into a heated pan,
flames began to rise. The whole room was aglow. I quickly
placed a lid on the pan to smother the fire. Today's Gospel
reminds us that faith is like oil. It's quite powerful. Just a
little bit can turn into a blazing flame.

1 Thessalonians 4:1–8
Psalm 97:1 and 2b, 5–6, 10, 11–12
Matthew 25:1–13

# AUGUST 29

*Nevertheless we urge you, brothers and sisters, to progress even more and to aspire to live a tranquil life, to mind your own affairs.*
—1 THESSALONIANS 4:11

My kids were in high school when our family suffered the trauma of divorce. We lived in a small town, so gossip spread quickly. I overheard two people speculating that the divorce was probably related to our child with special needs. Someone asked me how long I would stay in my home. "When the kids leave, your home will be too big for you," he said. In today's Scripture we read these words: "mind your own affairs." When we hear gossip, the most loving thing we can do is turn away. It's better if we pray for the private affairs of others. Then we can better mind our own.

1 Thessalonians 4:9–11
Psalm 98:1, 7–8, 9
Mark 6:17–29

# AUGUST 30

*"This people honors me with their lips, / but their hearts are far from me."*
—MARK 7:6

We've seen the politicians who are exposed on national television for their extramarital affairs. Their private sins are broadcast to the world. They are portrayed as hypocrites because their public words don't match their private dishonesty. But what if our own secret sins were recorded for all to see? What if thousands of viewers overheard our family arguments? What if our mean-spirited thoughts were documented in a magazine? Would others judge us as hypocritical? Fortunately, God forgives and forgets our sins. Each day we get another chance to make our lives right. All the more incentive to honor God with our words *and* our hearts.

Deuteronomy 4:1–2, 6–8
Psalm 15:2–3, 3–4, 4–5 (1a)
James 1:17–18, 21b–22, 27
Mark 7:1–8, 14–15, 21–23

*So that you do not grieve like the rest, who have no hope.*
—1 THESSALONIANS 4:13

When a person is grieving, it's hard to know what to say.
But our role, as comforters, is to be present to the
bereaved. A simple hug or clasping of a person's hand can
bring untold warmth to a despairing heart. Today, give
hope to someone in grief. You don't have to say a thing.

1 Thessalonians 4:13–18
Psalm 96:1 and 3, 4–5, 11–12, 13
Luke 4:16–30

# SEPTEMBER 1

*For all of you are children of the light.*
—1 THESSALONIANS 5:5

This past Sunday, I was asked to talk about creation to about seventy-five preschoolers. After gathering the kids around me, I turned off the lights and lit a large candle. "In the beginning it was dark and God said: 'Let there be light.'" The kids were quiet, mesmerized by the flame. In a hushed voice, I began telling them that God liked the light so much that he began creating other things. "What else did God make?" I asked them. Their boisterous answers came from all corners of the room: horses, fish, ants, flowers, leaves, pumpkins. Their joy was irrepressible. One little girl began dancing as she said, laughing, "God made pigs!" What would it take for us grown-ups to have such joy in God's creation?

1 Thessalonians 5:1–6, 9–11
Psalm 27:1, 4, 13–14
Luke 4:31–37

# SEPTEMBER 2

*At sunset, all who had people sick with various diseases brought them to him. He laid his hands on them and cured them.*

—LUKE 4:40

Every evening, something happens that many folks miss: the sun sets. The sky celebrates the merging of day and night. Breathtaking colors dangle between darkness and light. In today's Gospel, many people come to Jesus when the sun is setting. I see the Lord's face lit by the orange glow of the heavens. I see his hands, radiant with light, reaching out to heal the sick. It's such a beautiful image. Just before the darkness falls, the Light of the world shines.

Colossians 1:1–8
Psalm 52:10, 11
Luke 4:38–44

*Thursday*

# SEPTEMBER 3

• ST. GREGORY THE GREAT, POPE AND DOCTOR OF THE CHURCH •

*After he had finished speaking, he said to Simon, "Put out into deep water and lower your nets for a catch." Simon said in reply, "Master, we have worked hard all night and have caught nothing, but at your command I will lower the nets."*

—LUKE 5:4–5

The disciples are commanded to "put out into deep waters." Similarly, God often tells us to row into uncertain seas. When we feel a prompting to change something—whether it be a relationship, a job, or a location—it can feel as if we are drifting in an ocean. Will we run into storms? Will we get lost? The disciples discovered that great blessings are often hidden in unfamiliar places. Are you being called to the deep waters?

Colossians 1:9–14
Psalm 98:2–3ab, 3cd–4, 5–6
Luke 5:1–11

*Jesus answered them, "Can you make the wedding guests fast while the bridegroom is with them?"*
—LUKE 5:34

On a recent Saturday morning, I met my mother and all five of my sisters at a little lakeside deli. For a couple of hours, we laughed and reminisced. As we ate fattening desserts, I didn't worry about the calories I was consuming. With all of us getting older, our lives could be altered in an instant. This was a moment to celebrate our health, our family, and our immutable love for one another. Jesus understood the importance of embracing beautiful moments. He told his disciples to rejoice while the bridegroom was with them. Now is the time to celebrate.

Colossians 1:15–20
Psalm 100:1b–2, 3, 4, 5
Luke 5:33–39

*While Jesus was going through a field of grain on a sabbath, his disciples were picking the heads of grain, rubbing them in their hands, and eating them.*
—LUKE 6:1

When autumn arrives, I take an annual drive with a friend through northern Minnesota. From our car window, we see the wheat fields go on for miles. The stalks wave in the wind, glistening like strips of golden silk. Surrounded by wheat, I can easily picture Jesus "going through a field of grain on a Sabbath." I see him strolling through the fields, talking informally with his disciples. I see a band of brothers sharing the day, "picking the heads of grain." It's a peaceful scene. On the Sabbath day, do you take time for loved ones, or is it just another day to work in the field?

Colossians 1:21–23
Psalm 54:3–4, 6 and 8
Luke 6:1–5

# SEPTEMBER 6

*Say to those whose hearts are frightened: / Be strong, fear not!*
—ISAIAH 35:4

I once read that people's number-one fear is speaking in front of a group. In the minutes before I give a presentation, I always feel butterflies in my stomach. I breathe rapidly and can feel my heart beating quickly. But when I finally arrive at the podium, I feel a calmness. It's as if the Lord is saying, "It's my message. There is nothing to fear." What is your biggest fear? Can you envision God helping you conquer it?

Isaiah 35:4–7a
Psalm 146:6–7, 8–9, 9–10 (1b)
James 2:1–5
Mark 7:31–37

*On a certain sabbath Jesus went into the synagogue and taught, and
there was a man there whose right hand was withered.*
—LUKE 6:6

On the Sabbath, a man with a withered hand came to the
synagogue. He simply showed up. And Jesus restored his
hand. But what if the man had stayed home? What if he
had blamed God for his disability and refused to worship
him? Each weekend, we are invited to worship in a
community of faith. In the presence of other believers, we
can meet Jesus in word and sacrament. Through hymns,
quiet reflection, and Holy Communion, we can seek
restoration and healing. Miracles are worth showing up for.

Colossians 1:24—2:3
Psalm 62:6–7, 9
Luke 6:6–11

# SEPTEMBER 8

• THE NATIVITY OF THE BLESSED VIRGIN MARY •

*We know that all things work together for good for those who love God.*
—ROMANS 8:28

I've been reading a devotional book, *Hope*, by Nancy Guthrie. She relates the story of a young missionary family who was serving in Peru. In April 2001, the Peruvian air force opened fire on their small plane, mistaking them for drug runners. A bullet killed the young mother and her baby. At the funeral, the surviving husband spoke about forgiveness. He said that the bullet that struck his wife and child was a "sovereign bullet." And I thought, *No, God doesn't send suffering*. But then I remembered the sword that pierced Mary's heart and the nails that crucified Christ. We can't judge what is God's will and what isn't. But we can open our hearts to any good that God brings out of our trials.

Micah 5:1–4a or Romans 8:28–30
Psalm 13:6ab, 6c
Matthew 1:1–16, 18–23 or 1:18–23

*"Blessed are you who are now weeping, / for you will laugh."*
—LUKE 6:21

One winter morning, I had argued with my three daughters. Then I was driving them to school, the windshield wipers brushing away the snow. At a stoplight, our anger silently smoldered. But then we noticed the car in front of us. A passenger in the front seat seemed agitated. It looked like a large man wearing a fur hat with flaps. His head bobbed back and forth, and several times he lunged at the driver, an elderly man. "Mom, that guy looks abusive," said Rachael. After writing down the license plate, I pulled up to the side of the car. A long-eared dog stared back at us, panting happily. Laughter erupted in our minivan. Sometimes laughter comes more quickly than we expect.

Colossians 3:1–11
Psalm 145:2–3, 10–11, 12–13ab
Luke 6:20–26

# SEPTEMBER 10

*Put on, as God's chosen ones, holy and beloved, heartfelt compassion,*
*kindness, humility, gentleness, and patience, bearing with one another.*
—COLOSSIANS 3:13

Friends disappoint us. Family members bug us. Colleagues
get on our nerves. But the writer of Colossians tells us to
bear with one another. In this sense, the word *bear* means
"to forbear," or to "put up with" others. When we accept
the flaws of our brothers and sisters, we can better accept
our own. Today, I'd like to pass along a meditation that has
helped me learn to bear with others. Think of someone
who drives you crazy. Ask God for the patience to love
him or her, as God does. Call to mind your own
imperfections. Then pray, "Thank you, God, for putting
up with me."

Colossians 3:12–17
Psalm 150:1b–2, 3–4, 5–6
Luke 6:27–38

*"Can a blind person guide a blind person?"*
—LUKE 6:39

In 1886, a young teacher named Anne Sullivan arrived at the home of the Keller family. Little Helen was just six years old, both blind and deaf. One day, Anne began running cool water over Helen's fingers. The teacher began spelling the word *water* on the girl's hand. In a miraculous moment, the child made a connection between words and her world. Most people don't know that Anne was visually impaired, too. But Anne saw, with great clarity, the tenacity of Helen's spirit. Perhaps that's why Helen Keller was inspired to craft these unforgettable words: "The best and most beautiful things in the world cannot be seen or even touched—they must be felt with the heart."

1 Timothy 1:1–2, 12–14
Psalm 16:1b–2a and 5, 7–8, 11
Luke 6:39–42

# SEPTEMBER 12

• THE MOST HOLY NAME OF MARY •

*"But the one who listens and does not act is like a person who built a house on the ground without a foundation. When the river burst against it, it collapsed at once and was completely destroyed."*
—LUKE 6:48

A few summers back, a tornado destroyed homes in a nearby suburb. I remember visiting a friend who lived in the area. I was amazed that the newer homes in the development had sustained most of the damage. In contrast, the mid-century homes that framed the neighborhood had weathered the winds without incident. I overheard one resident say, "The older homes were made with better materials." Jesus tells us that developing our faith life is like building a solid home. We must use good materials: trust, hope, forgiveness, and love.

1 Timothy 1:15–17
Psalm 113:1b–2, 3–4, 5a and 6–7
Luke 6:43–49

# SEPTEMBER 13

• ST. JOHN CHRYSOSTOM •

*The Lord GOD opens my ear that I may hear.*
—ISAIAH 50:5

I've never heard God speak audibly. But I've definitely felt God's prompting. About six months before I moved to my current home, I started packing my belongings in cardboard boxes. I hadn't even found a new place. Even so, I had an overwhelming sense that a big change was coming. In my spirit, I kept hearing one word over and over again: *prepare.* Is God prompting you for a change? Is it time to prepare?

Isaiah 50:5–9a
Psalm 116:1–2, 3–4, 5–6, 8–9 (9)
James 2:14–18
Mark 8:27–35

*For God so loved the world.*
—JOHN 3:16

As I took my morning jog one day, I watched several young teenagers walking to the bus stop. All of them were wearing silly hats. It was Hat Day at the local middle school, an annual celebration that takes place each autumn. One boy wore an overstuffed Minnesota Vikings hat with horns. He had long skinny legs and pigeon-toed feet, and his hat was three times bigger than his head. As he raced to the bus stop, awkwardly, the hat began tilting to one side. I looked at him with the affection of a mother. *He's so dear*, I thought. God must feel the same way about us. Even in our awkward moments, God loves us dearly.

Numbers 21:4b–9
Psalm 78:1–2, 34–35, 36–37, 38
Philippians 2:6–11
John 3:13–17

# SEPTEMBER 15

• OUR LADY OF SORROWS •

*Whoever slanders his neighbor in secret, / him will I destroy.*
—PSALM 101:5

Gossip is usually shared in hushed tones. Slanderous secrets are often told behind closed doors. But today's Scripture tells us to beware of quiet conversations that defame a person's character. Idle gossip can easily turn into a slanderous attack. We can fan a flame of slander by simply listening to a story that may or may not be true. Or we can run from the heat. Today, avoid whispered conversations. Instead, tell an encouraging story out loud.

1 Timothy 3:1–13
Psalm 101:1b–2ab, 2cd–3ab, 5, 6
John 19:25–27 or Luke 2:33–35

# SEPTEMBER 16

• SS. CORNELIUS, POPE AND MARTYR, AND CYPRIAN, BISHOP AND MARTYR •

*I will give thanks to the LORD with all my heart, / in the company and assembly of the just.*
—PSALM 111:1

Lately, I've been doing more teaching in my church's Sunday-morning preschool program. Last Sunday, my role was to give assistance to a little boy with Down syndrome. About fifteen minutes into the hour, most of the children began following another teacher to another activity. But the boy in my charge hid behind the curtain of a small puppet stage. "We've got to be on our way," I told him. But through the curtain, I could see him happily placing a Big Bird puppet on his hand. Out came the yellow-beaked puppet. I pulled up a stool. The puppet began singing: "Go tell it on the mountain that Jesus Christ is born." Though the song was filled with stutters and long pauses, I was grateful for the performance. The Gospel was being proclaimed.

1 Timothy 3:14–16
Psalm 111:1–2, 3–4, 5–6
Luke 7:31–35

*Jesus said to him in reply, "Simon, I have something to say to you."*
—LUKE 7:40

At family gatherings, my mother's home can get pretty loud. Usually her kitchen and dining room are packed with my sisters, brothers, nieces, nephews, and all the in-laws. We never sit down for dinner. Instead, all of us graze on the potluck dishes that fill her kitchen table. But just before the grazing begins, my brother Terry yells, "Hey everybody!" That's our cue to stop talking and pay attention. It's the moment when Terry takes his place in the middle of us all and prays a simple prayer over the meal. When Jesus said to Simon, "I have something to say to you," it was Simon's cue to listen. I'm sure that Jesus has something to say to us, if only we pay attention.

1 Timothy 4:12–16
Psalm 111:7–8, 9, 10
Luke 7:36–50

*Friday*

# SEPTEMBER 18

*For we brought nothing into the world, just as we shall not be able to take anything out of it.*
—1 TIMOTHY 6:7

An ad for an estate sale often includes a phrase like "years of accumulation will be sold." Those words are sobering. It reminds me that the material blessings of this life are temporal. But is it sinful to have a comfortable home or nice clothing? The Scriptures tell us that God delights in providing us with these things. But our material blessings are not meant to be hoarded. When we share our homes, our cars, and all the other financial blessings we've been given, we are furthering the work of Christ. May we share freely and with great joy.

1 Timothy 6:2c–12
Psalm 49:6–7, 8–10, 17–18, 19–20
Luke 8:1–3

⇒ 293 ⇐

# SEPTEMBER 19

• ST. JANUARIUS, BISHOP AND MARTYR •

*"But as for the seed that fell on rich soil, they are the ones who, when they have heard the word, embrace it with a generous and good heart."*
—LUKE 8:15

When I was in the second grade, my class planted marigold seeds in small milk cartons filled with dirt. Near a bank of sunlit windows, the bright blossoms began sprouting just before Mother's Day. I was so proud to give my mother what I called my "miracle marigold." I just couldn't believe that a small seed had produced such loveliness, with its green leaves and bright orange petals. The plant was alive and growing, beautiful to behold. Jesus tells us that our faith is like a seed that grows in rich soil. When it blossoms, it's beautiful.

1 Timothy 6:13–16
Psalm 100:1b–2, 3, 4, 5
Luke 8:4–15

# SEPTEMBER 20

*You ask but do not receive, because you ask wrongly, to spend it
on your passions.*
—JAMES 4:3

If you are experiencing confusion in your prayer time, try
being still. In the quietness, let your ruminations become
like water trickling in a stream. Pay attention to the
thoughts and memories that drift past. Notice the pebbles
that shimmer in your dreams. Wade through past hurts.
Don't discount any of your reflections. Allow God to
clarify your thoughts. Let God show you what you need to
surrender or heal. In his holy presence, the right prayer
will come.

Wisdom 2:12, 17–20
Psalm 54:3–4, 5, 6–8 (6b)
James 3:16–4:3
Mark 9:30–37

# SEPTEMBER 21

• ST. MATTHEW, APOSTLE AND EVANGELIST •

*But grace was given to each of us.*
—EPHESIANS 4:7

William Blake's poem, "Auguries of Innocence" reads,

To see a World in a Grain of Sand
And a Heaven in a Wild Flower,
Hold Infinity in the palm of your hand
And Eternity in an hour.

Ephesians 4:1–7, 11–13
Psalm 19:2–3, 4–5
Matthew 9:9–13

# SEPTEMBER 22

*Let us go rejoicing to the house of the Lord.*
—PSALM 122:1

The Pew Research Center recently reported that only 41 percent of American Catholics attend Mass once a week. This rings true in my immediate family. Four of my siblings now attend evangelical and Protestant churches. My other siblings are deeply spiritual but feel no need to be part of organized religion. But we all agree on one thing: at our core, we are still Catholic. This is because the most sacred moments of our lives have been sealed within the walls of a Catholic church—every baptism, first communion, wedding, and funeral. The faith of our youth remains rooted in our hearts. Do the current statistics ring true in your network of family and friends? How do you respond when a loved one decides to leave the church?

Ezra 6:7–8, 12b, 14–20
Psalm 122:1–2, 3–4ab, 4cd–5
Luke 8:19–21

# SEPTEMBER 23

*I said: "My God, I am too ashamed and confounded to raise my
face to you."*
—EZRA 9:6

"Shame on you!" Frustrated parents sometimes use these
words when scolding a child. But an invocation of shame is
never helpful, especially when someone makes a mistake or
a poor decision. Shame breeds self-disgust and humiliation.
It's another way of saying, "You have failed miserably!"
Jesus wasn't interested in shaming sinners. When the
woman was caught in adultery, Jesus didn't hurl stones of
condemnation. He simply challenged her to change.
Shame, whether we heap it on ourselves or it is heaped on
us by others, will not lift us to a better way.

Ezra 9:5–9
Tobit 13:2, 3–4a, 4befghn, 7–8
Luke 9:1–6

# SEPTEMBER 24

*Now thus says the LORD of hosts: / Consider your ways!*
—HAGGAI 9:7

Centuries ago, St. Ignatius of Loyola crafted a five-step prayer called the Daily Examen. I use the prayer every evening; it's a great way to close my day. I begin by considering the day that has just passed. I ask myself a few questions: *Where did I see God's grace? Did I seize the opportunity to serve others? In what ways was I challenged to become more Christ-like? What needs to be healed?* As I examine my day with God, it feels as if I'm unearthing the sacredness that may be buried in my busy life. And I'm ready to do it all again, tomorrow, if God wills. How are you taking time to "consider" your life?

Haggai 1:1–8
Psalm 149:1b–2, 3–4, 5–6a and 9b
Luke 9:7–9

# SEPTEMBER 25

*Greater will be the future glory of this house / than the former, says the LORD of hosts.*
—HAGGAI 2:9

I was dismayed when my dentist told me that I needed a crown and some other expensive work. "I can only afford to do the crown," I told him. He nodded knowingly. Then he said, "You never know what will happen with your finances. Things could change tomorrow." When I left his office, I wasn't worried about my dental bill. I was dreaming about the future. Maybe I was about to secure a new book contract or receive an unexpected financial provision. You never know. God says that our future will be greater than our past. When we place our trust in God, anything can happen.

Haggai 2:1–9
Psalm 43:1, 2, 3, 4
Luke 9:18–22

*I will console and gladden them after their sorrows.*
—JEREMIAH 31:13

We can never be separated from the consolation of Christ.
The word *console* means "to comfort," "to reassure," or "to
soothe." How has the Lord consoled you?

Zechariah 2:5–9, 14–15a
Jeremiah 31:10, 11–12ab, 13
Luke 9:43b–45

# SEPTEMBER 27

*Anyone who gives you a cup of water to drink because you belong to Christ, amen, I say to you, will surely not lose his reward.*
—MARK 9:41

Not long ago, a nineteen-year-old boy from Minnesota made national news. Newscasters reported that Joey Prusak was working at Dairy Queen when a blind man came into his store and dropped a twenty-dollar bill. A woman picked up the bill and tucked it into her purse. Joey asked her to return the money to the man. "It's mine," the woman said. She began swearing at Joey. "I'm not going to serve you if you're going to be disrespectful," Joey said. The woman stormed out of the store. Employees and patrons watched Joey take a twenty-dollar bill from his own wallet and give it to the disabled man. Joey's example sheds light on today's Gospel reading. In the kingdom of God, our small deeds of kindness make a big difference.

Numbers 11:25–29
Psalm 19:8, 10, 12–13, 14 (9a)
James 5:1–6
Mark 9:38–43, 45, 47–48

# SEPTEMBER 28

*"For the one who is least among all of you is the one who is
the greatest."*
—LUKE 9:48

Every Christmas morning, our family invites to breakfast
two sisters who are disabled. The women are in their early
fifties, disheveled, and loud. They usually spill hot
chocolate on my rugs and burp at our dining room table.
But they've warmed their way into our hearts. Every year,
they buy us presents at the Goodwill store and wrap them
in newspaper and masking tape. (I always get hot pads!)
My daughters have developed a special fondness for our
guests. "It's doesn't feel like Christmas until they come," my
youngest recently said. I feel that we have been visited
by Christ.

Zechariah 8:1–8
Psalm 102:16–18, 19–21, 29 and 22–23
Luke 9:46–50

# SEPTEMBER 29

• SS. MICHAEL, GABRIEL, AND RAPHAEL, ARCHANGELS •

*Nathanael said to him, "How do you know me?" Jesus answered and said to him, "Before Philip called you, I saw you under the fig tree."*
—JOHN 1:48

You are known by God. God is acquainted with the conflicts you face each day. He remembers what happened yesterday in your life. He sees your secret sins and forgives them. He understands all your fears, hopes, and dreams. How does it make you feel to be known so intimately by God? Do you feel unsettled that nothing in your life is hidden from God? Or are you comforted that God will never stop loving you?

Daniel 7:9–10, 13–14 or Revelation 12:7–12ab
Psalm 138:1–2ab, 2cde–3, 4–5
John 1:47–51

Wednesday

# SEPTEMBER 30

• ST. JEROME, PRIEST AND DOCTOR OF THE CHURCH •

*The king granted my requests, for the favoring hand of my God was upon me.*
—NEHEMIAH 2:8

In the moments that followed the birth of my first baby, the doctor placed her in my arms. In quiet awe, I watched our newborn curl her hand around my index finger. I was shocked at the immediate love I felt for this little person. In that instant, I knew I could lay down my life for her. Most new parents can relate to this image. The clasp of parent and child captures the enormity of God's love for us. Each day, his hand reaches out to us. We can choose to ignore his enormous tenderness. Or we can curl our hand around his index finger. In the grip of grace, God's favor rests.

Nehemiah 2:1–8
Psalm 137:1–2, 3, 4–5, 6
Luke 9:57–62

*Thursday*

# OCTOBER 1

• ST. THÉRÈSE OF THE CHILD JESUS, VIRGIN AND DOCTOR OF THE CHURCH •

*"Hush, for today is holy, and you must not be saddened."*
—NEHEMIAH 8:9

Self-talk helped me through my daughter's terminal illness. Each morning, when I would imagine the future without Sarah, I would say, "Not today." Then I would celebrate the day. My precious child was alive, and so were her two sisters. We made peanut-butter bars and painted our toenails. We ordered yummy drinks at the coffee shop and danced in the kitchen. We cranked up the radio and sang off-key. We watched videos, paged through scrapbooks, held hands, and laughed. Yes, the awful day came when Sarah passed away. And many sad days followed. But hope has replaced the worst of my grief. Does your future hold an unchangeable challenge? Try to say, "Not today." Don't miss the joy.

Nehemiah 8:1–4a, 5–6, 7b–12
Psalm 19:8, 9, 10, 11
Luke 10:1–12

# OCTOBER 2

• THE HOLY GUARDIAN ANGELS •

*From the time the Lord led our ancestors out of the land of Egypt until
the present day, we have been disobedient to the Lord, our God, and
only too ready to disregard his voice.*

—BARUCH 1:19

We've all broken a commandment or two, or more. But
while we should always strive to follow God's mandates,
true faith requires more from us. Faith, at its core, is about
companionship with God, who desires to be in
relationship with us. He longs to share intimate
conversations through daily prayer and worship. He is
always ready to forgive. Yes, God is the omnipotent giver
of the law, worthy of our respect and obedience. But in
Christ he is also our humble friend.

Baruch 1:15–22
Psalm 79:1b–2, 3–5, 8, 9
Matthew 18:1–5, 10

# OCTOBER 3

_The seventy-two disciples returned rejoicing and said to Jesus, "Lord,
even the demons are subject to us because of your name."_
—LUKE 10:17

When I was in high school, all my friends wanted me to go
see the movie _The Exorcist._ I never went—I was too afraid. I
didn't want to watch frightful images of demons and evil
spirits. I was especially afraid of watching two priests
perform an exorcism on a twelve-year-old girl. But today's
passage gives me a new perspective on the powers of
darkness. The disciples have just discovered that the name
of Jesus dispels demons. They are rejoicing. I can see them
smiling, laughing, maybe even dancing. I can almost hear
them saying, "Lord, all we did was use your name." Only
one name, uttered in confidence, repels evil: _Jesus._

Baruch 4:5–12, 27–29
Psalm 69:33–35, 36–37
Luke 10:17–24

# OCTOBER 4

*"Amen I say to you, whoever does not accept the kingdom of God like a child will not enter it." Then he embraced them and blessed them, placing his hands on them.*
—MARK 10:15

Every morning, my little daughters would ask, "What are we going to do today, Mom?" I always had something planned. I knew that if the kids had activities in the morning, they would take long naps in the afternoon. Some mornings we swam at the pool or read books at the library. Other days we biked around the lake or visited a museum. We never did anything extraordinary. We simply spent time together. But now that my children are grown, they often say, "Those were some of the best days of our lives." Jesus longs to spend the same kind of time with us. There's no need to plan anything extraordinary. Just being together is enough.

Genesis 2:18–24
Psalm 128:1–2, 3, 4–5, 6
Hebrews 2:9–11
Mark 10:2–16 or 10:2–12

# OCTOBER 5

*But because he wished to justify himself, he said to Jesus, "And who is my neighbor?"*
—LUKE 10:29

At five o'clock this morning, I was on the treadmill. As I jogged, a woman walked past the window. Though it was early, she was wearing a radiant smile and a T-shirt that read "Warning! Praise Zone." On her shirt was the graphic of a traffic sign and a silhouette of a person with raised hands. I waved to her. She waved back and went happily on her way. Jogging onward, I smiled. She, my neighbor, was a fellow pilgrim on the journey of faith. As you go through your days on the earth, be sure to wave at your neighbors. You'll find them everywhere.

Jonah 1:1–2:1, 2, 11
Jonah 2:3, 4, 5, 8
Luke 10:25–37

# OCTOBER 6

• ST. BRUNO, PRIEST • BLESSED MARIE-ROSE DUROCHER, VIRGIN •

*Jesus entered a village where a woman whose name was Martha
welcomed him. She had a sister named Mary.*
—LUKE 10:38

Usually, when we hear the story of Mary and Martha, we
think of Mary as the "good" sister. After all, she chose to sit
at the feet of Jesus while Martha busied herself with meal
preparations. But before the conflict between the sisters
surfaced, Martha welcomed Jesus. The busy, preoccupied
sister took a moment to offer hospitality. Maybe she gave
Jesus a warm smile or offered him a cool drink. Maybe she
said something like, "My Lord, I'm so happy you have
come. I've fixed you a special dinner." Martha shows us just
how important hospitality is. Even when we are busy, we
can make Jesus feel welcome.

Jonah 3:1–10
Psalm 130:1b–2, 3–4ab, 7–8
Luke 10:38–42

*But the LORD asked, "Have you reason to be angry?"*
—JONAH 4:4

When we experience an unexpected loss, it's natural to feel angry. But is it irreverent to clench our fists at God? Will God turn away if we kick and shout? When we express our true feelings to God, we validate the intimacy of our friendship. We give him our whole selves, not just part of us. We hide nothing from him. Do you have reason to be angry with God? Make that part of your prayer; God can handle the truth.

Jonah 4:1–11
Psalm 86:3–4, 5–6, 9–10
Luke 11:1–4

# OCTOBER 8

*What father among you would hand his son a snake when he
asks for a fish?*
—LUKE 11:11

What do you need from God today? Do you need healing
from an illness, provisions for your family, a new attitude,
clarity about a decision, hope, friendship, or simply the
strength to survive another day? Our loving Father is
interested in hearing our specific requests. With great
compassion, God will hand us what we need.

Malachi 3:13–20b
Psalm 1:1–2, 3, 4 and 6
Luke 11:5–13

*"Proclaim a fast, / call an assembly; / Gather the elders, / all who dwell
in the land."*
—JOEL 13:14

Food is everywhere in our culture. In a typical grocery
store, the bread aisle is packed with muffins, bagels, and
loaves. At midnight, we can drive to a window and be
served a cheeseburger. Television chefs tell us how to
prepare pasta, desserts, and drinks. But there are certain
times when we must proclaim a fast. For example, when we
are facing a huge decision, a fast is appropriate. When we
deny ourselves food, God can nourish us with wisdom and
clarity. As we turn away from the groceries in our
cupboard, God can lead us to his will.

Joel 1:13–15; 2:1–2
Psalm 9:2–3, 6 and 16, 8–9
Luke 11:15–26

*"Rather, blessed are those who hear the word of God and observe it."*
—LUKE 11:28

It takes discipline to observe the word of God. It's not enough to just hear the Scriptures; when we open the Bible, we are called to savor the Scriptures like fine food. We must digest each passage slowly. To really know God, we must contemplate the story, examine the words, and ponder the teachings. Only then can we put this sacred word into practice. Do you want to build a better relationship with God? Try to spend more quality time with Scripture.

Joel 4:12–21
Psalm 97:1–2, 5–6, 11–12
Luke 11:27–28

*Indeed the word of God is living and effective, sharper than any
two-edged sword.*
—HEBREWS 4:12

Imagine a blade with two sharp edges. Its purpose is to cut
both ways. In today's reading, the word of the Lord is
compared to this powerful weapon. Like a sword, the
commandments of God slice away sin. These holy
lacerations are painful for us because it's never easy to feel
the sting of our transgressions and the ache we have
caused others. But God's word has an equally important
purpose. It cuts a sacred opening in our heart, a space that
can hold his unconditional mercy and love. When have
you felt this holy, double-edged sword?

Wisdom 7:7–11
Psalm 90:12–13, 14–15, 16–17 (14)
Hebrews 4:12–13
Mark 10:17–30 or 10:17–27

# OCTOBER 12

*Sing to the LORD a new song, / for he has done wondrous deeds.*
—PSALM 98:1

The Eagles' song "Take It Easy" was popular back in the mid-1970s, when I was in high school. Sometimes, when my friends and I drove to parties, the song would be playing on the radio. I can still remember a carload of teenage voices belting out the lyrics. All these years later, when I hear the song, carefree memories of my youth return. Songs of praise can bring to mind special memories, too. Every time I hear "Amazing Grace," I think about all the ways God has sustained me. Is there a song or hymn that is dear to you? Can you sing it right now?

Romans 1:1–7
Psalm 98:1, 2–3ab, 3cd–4
Luke 11:29–32

# OCTOBER 13

*They exchanged the truth of God for a lie.*
—ROMANS 1:25

Alcoholic people often deny that they have a problem. But
when a drinker is confronted in an intervention, he or she
hears the truth. Family and friends will tell the person,
"Your drinking has hurt us. You need help." Fortunately,
many alcoholics enter a treatment program and find
positive ways to change. But if a person refuses to get help,
he or she can end up living a life of lies and loneliness.
Jesus wants us to be honest in all areas of our lives. If God
were to host an intervention in your life, what area would
he confront?

Romans 1:16–25
Psalm 19:2–3, 4–5
Luke 11:37–41

*Wednesday*

# OCTOBER 14

• ST. CALLISTUS I, POPE AND MARTYR •

*"You love the seat of honor in synagogues and greetings*
*in marketplaces."*
—LUKE 11:43

When one of my children had serious health issues, our family sat in the back pew of our church. There, in a small alcove, we were surrounded by a little community of people with disabilities. Over those difficult months, our family got to know the elderly, the sick, and several children with mental challenges. During the sign of peace, we hugged one another as if we were longtime friends. When the eucharistic ministers brought us communion, I remember being hemmed in by wheelchairs, walkers, and picture boards. It was a beautiful feeling. God's love shone in the eyes and smiles of our special friends. There are many seats of honor in our churches. But sometimes, the best seats are in the back row.

Romans 2:1–11
Psalm 62:2–3, 6–7, 9
Luke 11:42–46

*I trust in the LORD; / my soul trusts in his word.*
—PSALM 130:5

I have a friend who never locks her car when there are groceries in the backseat. "If someone needs food, God wants them to have it," she once told me. My friend is living out her faith in a powerful way. Without any words, she is proclaiming, "Even my food belongs to the Lord." It's an image of complete trust and surrender. Can you trust the Lord with your groceries? Your car? Your life?

Romans 3:21–30
Psalm 130:1b–2, 3–4, 5–6ab
Luke 11:47–54

*Friday*

# OCTOBER 16

• ST. HEDWIG, RELIGIOUS • ST. MARGARET MARY ALACOQUE, VIRGIN •

*Therefore whatever you have said in the darkness will be heard in the light.*
—LUKE 12:3

When I share a secret with a friend, it's no longer a secret. My private story then belongs to someone I trust. Likewise, Jesus knows the truths that are hidden in our hearts. He is our truest friend. We can trust that our secrets are safe with him.

Romans 4:1–8
Psalm 32:1b–2, 5, 11
Luke 12:1–7

*"For the Holy Spirit will teach you at the moment what you should say."*
—LUKE 12:12

There was a time when I didn't know what to say at a funeral. I always thought I needed to pass along an eloquent quote or write a long poetic verse on a card. But I know now that only two words are necessary: "I'm sorry." Those two simple words can offer so much comfort and compassion.

Romans 4:13, 16–18
Psalm 105:6–7, 8–9, 42–43
Luke 12:8–12

# OCTOBER 18

*Let us confidently approach the throne of grace.*
—HEBREW 4:16

When I was a young mom, I attended a weekly Bible study at a nearby church. One mother in the group was in charge of offering our opening prayer. She always began with the same words: "Lord, this morning we come to your throne." What comes to mind when you hear those words? Do you see yourself bowing before your heavenly King? Do you imagine the crown that adorns the head of your Savior? Can you hear the angels singing praise to God? Take a moment today to imagine that you are at the throne of the loving King who will treat you with fairness and compassion. You can approach God's throne with confidence, not fear.

Isaiah 53:10–11
Psalm 33:4–5, 18–19, 20, 22 (22)
Hebrews 4:14–16
Mark 10:35–45 or 10:42–45

*Monday*

# OCTOBER 19

• SS. JOHN DE BRÉBEUF AND ISAAC JOGUES, PRIESTS AND MARTYRS,
AND COMPANIONS, MARTYRS •

*"You fool, this night your life will be demanded of you; and the things
you have prepared, to whom will they belong? Thus will it be for the
one who stores up treasure for himself but is not rich in what
matters to God."*
—LUKE 12:20

There are five hundred twenty-five thousand six hundred
minutes in a year. How are you using those minutes? Are
you living a life that reflects the teachings of Jesus? Do you
love and forgive others? Are you growing from your losses?
Do you laugh, cry, sing, and dance? Are you sharing your
treasures? Today's reading reminds us that our days on the
earth will come to an end. We must use our minutes wisely.
The only treasures we will take with us are the riches of a
well-lived life.

Romans 4:20–25
Luke 1:69–70, 71–72, 73–75
Luke 12:13–21

*Tuesday*

# OCTOBER 20

• ST. PAUL OF THE CROSS, PRIEST •

*Blessed are those servants whom the master finds vigilant on his arrival.*
*Amen, I say to you, he will gird himself, have them recline at table, and*
*proceed to wait on them.*
—LUKE 12:37

There will be an astounding reward for those who serve
God. Jesus will prepare a feast for us. When all our work
on the earth is complete, we will sit down at a table he has
set. Jesus will be dressed for the occasion and he, himself,
will wait on us. It's hard to imagine what that dinner will be
like. Will it be uncomfortable to be served by Jesus? I'm
envisioning myself saying, "No, Lord, let me wait on you."
But then I recall what Jesus once told his disciples: "I have
called you friends" (John 15:15).

Romans 5:12, 15b, 17–19, 20b–21
Psalm 40:7–8a, 8b–9, 10, 17
Luke 12:35–38

⇒ 325 ⇐

# OCTOBER 21

*Much will be required of the person entrusted with much.*
—LUKE 12:48

A few years ago, a young mother was a columnist for my local Catholic newspaper. As I followed her writings, I often thought, *She has such potential.* It was obvious she had a gift. Her reflections always highlighted the important things in life: family, friendship, and faith. She died of cancer in her mid-thirties. As I ponder today's Scripture, I find myself thinking of her. Though her time on the earth was short, she used the gift that God had entrusted to her.

I imagine that God welcomed her to heaven with the words: "Well done, good and faithful servant!" What gift has God entrusted to you?

Romans 6:12–18
Psalm 124:1b–3, 4–6, 7–8
Luke 12:39–48

*Jesus said to his disciples: "I have come to set the earth on fire, and how I wish it were already blazing."*
—LUKE 12:49

When I start a fire in our fireplace, I often use the prepackaged "cheater logs" that are available at department stores. At the touch of a match, a log will blaze brightly. Last week, my daughter decided to light two logs at the same time. (She didn't know the packaging warned against this). Suddenly, my entire fireplace was filled with fire. When we closed the fireplace doors, the glass panes turned brown. Eventually the flames calmed down. At Pentecost, tongues of fire were seen above the heads of the disciples. As they began sharing the Gospel, the flame of the Holy Spirit blazed within them. Does the Holy Spirit flicker in you, or does it blaze like a mighty fire?

Romans 6:19–23
Psalm 1:1–2, 3, 4 and 6
Luke 12:49–53

*Never will I forget your precepts, / for through them you give me life.*
—PSALM 119:93

I'm steeped in Catholic tradition, and so I should be able to recite the Ten Commandments by heart. But sometimes I forget the exact wording. And I don't always remember the proper sequence of these sacred precepts. I'm not worried, though. Like every Christian, my conscience is a chalkboard on which the laws of God are written. I always know when I am sinning. When I am not following God's way, I don't sleep very well. If you can't recite the Ten Commandments, don't be dismayed. You'll find them written in your heart.

Romans 7:18–25a
Psalm 119:66, 68, 76, 77, 93, 94
Luke 12:54–59

# OCTOBER 24

*"Sir, leave it for this year also, and I shall cultivate the ground around it and fertilize it; it may bear fruit in the future."*
—LUKE 13:8

Have you been praying for someone's restoration? Are you frustrated that no answer has come? Maybe your prayers are bearing fruit in a way you cannot see. Like the fig tree in today's Gospel, maybe God is quietly cultivating the soil of healing. Perhaps branches are being pruned in the life of your loved one. As you wait for God's response, trust that your prayers will be answered. At just the right time, fruit will come.

Romans 8:1–11
Psalm 24:1b–2, 3–4ab, 5–6
Luke 13:1–9

*And many rebuked him, telling him to be silent. But he kept calling out all the more, "Son of David, have pity on me."*
—MARK 10:48

I don't know any author who hasn't had a manuscript rejected. But rejection isn't necessarily a bad thing. Years ago, I entered a writing contest. The prize was a trip to New York and a paid writing retreat with some of the best writers in Christian publishing. When I received word that I hadn't won, I spent a few moments sobbing. Then I began rewriting the story I had submitted. The rejection made me work harder. In the end, I became a better writer. In today's Gospel, a blind man is rebuked for calling out to the Lord. Is he silenced by the rejection? No! He calls out "all the more" to Jesus. If you are experiencing rejection, don't lose heart.

Jeremiah 31:7–9
Psalm 126:1–2, 2–3, 4–5, 6 (3)
Hebrews 5:1–6
Mark 10:46–52

# OCTOBER 26

*When Jesus saw her, he called to her and said, "Woman, you are set free of your infirmity." He laid his hands on her and she at once stood up straight and glorified God.*
—LUKE 13:13

This short passage is among my favorites. When I read it, I remember what my life was like a few years ago. Like the woman in today's story, I was bent over, weighed down with all that was unfolding in my life: a divorce, my daughter's illness, and the grief of losing a child. Have you been there? Have you been bent over with the heaviness of life? Today, imagine Jesus laying his hand upon you. Feel his power and hope. Let him help you stand up straight.

Romans 8:12–17
Psalm 68:2 and 4, 6–7ab, 20–21
Luke 13:10–17

# OCTOBER 27

*I consider that the sufferings of this present time are as nothing.*
—ROMANS 8:18

One of my friends is a pediatric cardiologist. She works
with children who have serious heart defects, most of them
life-threatening ones. Once I asked her, "Isn't it hard to see
children suffer, day after day?" She smiled and said, "I've
been trained to heal. Most of my little patients go home.
That's something to celebrate." Her words remind me of
today's reading. Our sufferings on earth are temporary.
Someday we will go home to Jesus, completely healed in
body, mind, and soul. That's something to celebrate!

Romans 8:18–25
Psalm 126:1b–2ab, 2cd–3, 4–5, 6
Luke 13:18–21

*Wednesday*

# OCTOBER 28

• SS. SIMON AND JUDE, APOSTLES •

*Jesus went up to the mountain to pray, and he spent the night in prayer to God.*
—LUKE 6:12

Have you ever had a restless night? Instead of lamenting about the sleep you are losing, why not spend the night praying? Give God all your worries and cares. Pray for your family members, one by one. Ask for discernment about upcoming decisions. If you think about it, the night holds endless possibilities for prayer.

Ephesians 2:19–22
Psalm 19:2–3, 4–5
Luke 6:12–16

# OCTOBER 29

*For I am convinced that neither death, nor life, nor angels, nor principalities, nor present things, nor future things, nor powers, nor height, nor depth, nor any other creature will be able to separate us from the love of God in Christ Jesus our Lord.*
—ROMANS 8:38–39

If you feel far from the Lord, try writing this verse on a small card. Tape it to your fridge, your bathroom mirror, or your dashboard. When you feel God's absence, read the verse out loud. Remind yourself of the truth. You are not alone. God is with you. Nothing can diminish God's love for you.

Romans 8:31b–39
Psalm 109:21–22, 26–27, 30–31
Luke 13:31–35

# OCTOBER 30

*I speak the truth in Christ, I do not lie.*
—ROMANS 9:1

My friends know that I'm not good at returning phone calls. Sometimes, when I'm very busy, it takes a day or two for me to get back to them. But a few months ago, my friend Roxy got fed up with me: "It's not good to put your friends on hold." I knew she was right. But the truth meant I had to change. I'm now working on being a better communicator. These days, when Roxy leaves a message on my voice mail, I try to call her right back. It's a small way of saying that I value our friendship. Do your friends confront you with the truth? How do you respond?

Romans 9:1–5
Psalm 147:12–13, 14–15, 19–20
Luke 14:1–6

# OCTOBER 31

*But the one who humbles himself will be exalted.*
—LUKE 14:11

We have many daily opportunities to be humble. We can give up our parking space. We can let another person go ahead of us in the checkout line. We can open a door, chat with a stranger, or greet someone who is quite different from us. These small actions have eternal significance. In heaven Jesus will acknowledge the simple ways we have honored the needs of others. Those who have humbled themselves on earth will be exalted forever.

Romans 11:1–2a, 11–12, 25–29
Psalm 94:12–13a, 14–15, 17–18
Luke 14:1, 7–11

*Beloved: See what love the Father has bestowed on us that we may be*
*called the children of God. Yet so we are.*
—1 JOHN 3:1

How would your life be different if you believed that God
was in love with you? Would you have more joy? Would
you trust God as a child trusts his or her mother or father?
Would you start believing that God cares for you more
than for the flowers or sparrows? Meditate on the word
*beloved.* What comes to mind?

Revelation 7:2–4, 9–14
Psalm 24:1–2, 3–4, 5–6
1 John 3:1–3
Matthew 5:1–12a

*For this is the will of my Father, that everyone who sees the Son and believes in him may have eternal life, and I shall raise him on the last day.*
—JOHN 6:40

Just before my grandmother passed away, she was resting in her bedroom. Though her breathing was labored, she turned her eyes toward a sunlit window. With a smile, she calmly said, "It's so beautiful. There are colors I've never seen before." Then she closed her eyes and died. I like to believe that my grandmother was catching her first glimpse of heaven. There's part me that wishes she had said more. I want to know all the details about eternity. But the glories of heaven were meant to be a surprise. Eternity is God's greatest gift, a present we must wait to open.

Wisdom 3:1–9
Psalm 23:1–3a, 3b–4, 5, 6 (1) (4ab) or 25:6 and 7b,
17–18, 20–21 or 27:1, 4, 7 and 8b and 9a, 13–14
Romans 5:5–11 or 6:3–9
John 6:37–40

# NOVEMBER 3

• ST. MARTIN DE PORRES, RELIGIOUS •

*LORD, my heart is not proud.*
—PSALM 131:1

Jesus calls us to follow his example of humility. Though he was God, he knelt before the disciples and washed their feet. We too must kneel before our brothers and sisters in Christ. This might mean surrendering our selfishness to God. When a heart is filled with the humility of Christ, there will be no room for selfish pride.

Romans 12:5–16ab
Psalm 131:1bcde, 2, 3
Luke 14:15–24

# NOVEMBER 4

• ST. CHARLES BORROMEO, BISHOP •

*Whoever does not carry his own cross and come after me cannot be my disciple.*
—LUKE 14:27

If someone was able to predict your future, would you want to know what it held? I think I'd like to catch a glimpse of the good things that lay ahead. I'd like to know who my children will marry or how many grandchildren I will have. But I don't want to know about the sufferings that might unfold in the years to come. If I could see my future trials, I would say, "No, God, I can't carry those crosses." Yet if adversity should come, God's shoulders are broad and strong. God is an experienced cross carrier, well versed in suffering. If you or I should fall beneath the weight of a cross, we need not despair.

Romans 13:8–10
Psalm 112:1b–2, 4–5, 9
Luke 14:25–33

# NOVEMBER 5

*"This man welcomes sinners and eats with them."*
—LUKE 15:2

Jesus ate dinner with sinners. If you were to follow Jesus' example, which "sinner" would you eat a meal with? Perhaps you are warring with a deceitful coworker or an insensitive friend. Maybe someone has wronged you in an egregious way. If it's difficult to imagine breaking bread with the sinners in your life, remember that Jesus made a point of eating with people considered detestable.

Romans 14:7–12
Psalm 27:1bcde, 4, 13–14
Luke 15:1–10

*I myself am convinced about you, my brothers and sisters, that you
yourselves are full of goodness.*
—ROMANS 15:14

Sadie was a good dog, my friend Mary's beloved golden
retriever. A regal creature, Sadie had kind eyes and seemed
to have a soul. In the months that followed my daughter's
death, I would often visit Mary. When I arrived at her
home, Sadie would retrieve a shoe for me and gently place
it at my feet. In Sadie's presence, I felt comforted. The
months passed and I slowly began to heal. But Sadie got
cancer and, a tumor began growing beneath her eye. On
the day Sadie passed away, I dropped by Mary's house to
say good-bye. "She can't see very well," Mary said.
Nonetheless, Sadie rose from her slumber and brought me
a shoe. "Thank you," I whispered. Sadie's life was a
testimony to goodness. Ours can be too.

Romans 15:14–21
Psalm 98:1, 2–3ab, 3cd–4
Luke 16:1–8

# NOVEMBER 7

*The person who is trustworthy in very small matters is also trustworthy in great ones.*
—LUKE 16:10

I once lost my cell phone while jogging around a lake. When I got home from my jog, I looked into my empty pocket and panicked. It was unsettling to think that all my contact information was sitting on the shoreline. But about an hour later, my daughter Christina dropped by my home. Much to my surprise, she handed me my cell phone. Apparently, a trustworthy woman had found my phone lying at the base of a bush. The stranger had searched my contact list and found my daughter's phone number. "Mom, the lady was so nice. She said she was glad to help." Today, look for ways to be trustworthy in small matters.

Romans 16:3–9, 16, 22–27
Psalm 145:2–3, 4–5, 10–11
Luke 16:9–15

# NOVEMBER 8

*"The jar of flour shall not go empty, nor the jug of oil run dry."*
—1 KING 17:14

Most financial experts suggest that each of us should have
at least six months of living expenses in our savings
account. We should also have an emergency fund. Over
the course of my life, I've tried to follow these basic
financial practices, but at times, my savings have dwindled
to nothing. God has provided for our family in times of
need. The prophet Elijah tells a poor widow, "The jar of
flour shall not go empty." If you are struggling with
finances, imagine yourself holding a jar. Ask God to fill it
with faith and all the provisions you need for today.

1 Kings 17:10–16
Psalm 146:7, 8–9, 9–10 (1b)
Hebrews 9:24–28
Mark 12:38–44 or 12:41–44

# NOVEMBER 9

• THE DEDICATION OF THE LATERAN BASILICA IN ROME •

*"Zeal for your house will consume me."*
—JOHN 2:17

Oscar Romero was the bishop of the Catholic Church in El Salvador. A champion of the poor, he was assassinated on March 24, 1980, while celebrating Mass at a small chapel. Just one day earlier, he had given a sermon in which he called on Salvadoran soldiers to obey God and stop oppressing the poor. Like Jesus, Oscar Romero had a zeal for truth and holiness that consumed him, even to his death. Where do you experience zeal for holiness?

Ezekiel 47:1–2, 8–9, 12
Psalm 46:2–3, 5–6, 8–9
1 Corinthians 3:9c–11, 16–17
John 2:13–22

# NOVEMBER 10

• ST. LEO THE GREAT, POPE AND DOCTOR OF THE CHURCH •

*"When you have done all you have been commanded, say, 'We are unprofitable servants; we have done what we were obliged to do.'"*
—LUKE 17:10

As believers, what are we obliged to do? Most Christians would agree that the Ten Commandments provide good parameters for living a holy life. But if we become robotic followers of the law, it's possible to become judgmental of those we perceive as not following the law. Jesus said that the greatest commandment was to love God and others. In other words, our greatest, and most holy obligation is to love.

Wisdom 2:23–3:9
Psalm 34:2–3, 16–17, 18–19
Luke 17:7–10

*As he was entering a village, ten lepers met him. They stood at a distance from him and raised their voice, saying, "Jesus, Master! Have pity on us!"*
—LUKE 17:12

After my divorce eleven years ago, I wondered if God still loved me. At that time, I could easily relate to the lepers in today's story. In their unhealed state, they couldn't draw near to Jesus. But from a distance they called out to him: "Jesus, Master! Have pity on us." The Lord heard their cries. So, too, the Lord heard the cries of this very imperfect divorcée. Through prayer, God's grace and healing has come. Today, if you feel far from God, try calling out to him as the lepers did. It's OK if you stand at a distance; God will still hear you.

Wisdom 6:1–11
Psalm 82:3–4, 6–7
Luke 17:11–19

*In Wisdom is a spirit, / intelligent, holy, unique.*
—WISDOM 7:22

In kindergarten, I was the last to learn how to tie my shoes. In grade school, I struggled with math and took special classes. In college, I took a biology course three times before I finally passed the class. I still don't feel very smart, but I've learned that spiritual intelligence is a gift to be celebrated. When God gives us wisdom, our thoughts are aligned with God's. We become tenderhearted, equipped to bear the pain of others. When we are wise, we will speak the truth with confidence. We will be drawn to the meek of the earth and share, freely, the love of Christ. Are you spiritually intelligent? Consider yourself smart.

Wisdom 7:22b–8:1
Psalm 119:89, 90, 91, 130, 135, 175
Luke 17:20–25

# NOVEMBER 13

*As it was in the days of Noah, so it will be in the days of the Son of Man; they were eating and drinking, marrying and giving in marriage.*
—LUKE 17:26–27

This morning, when I visited my Facebook page, I noticed that my daughter had posted several photos of a recent family wedding. There were about twenty pictures on the page—happy snapshots of my siblings, nieces, and nephews. The photos captured an unforgettable day. We were all smiling, dancing, celebrating the love of two very special kids. It was a day that we will treasure for many years to come. Jesus tells us he will come when people are "eating and drinking, marrying and giving in marriage." The passage implies that God will come when we least expect it. But if Jesus comes when we are cherishing the gift of love, we will be more than ready to meet him.

Wisdom 13:1–9
Psalm 19:2–3, 4–5ab
Luke 17:26–37

# NOVEMBER 14

*"But when the Son of Man comes, will he find faith on earth?"*
—LUKE 18:8

I often feel discouraged while watching the evening news. Night after night, there are stories of school shootings, murders, bombings, economic downturns, and woes in Washington. I sometimes wonder how much longer this world can survive. But then I remember that there are millions of faith-filled people in the world. People who are quietly praying for peace. People who sacrifice to care for others. Parents who are raising their kids to be kind and honest citizens. The nightly news doesn't recognize the simple, understated faith of ordinary believers.

But God does.

Wisdom 18:14–16; 19:6–9
Psalm 105:2–3, 36–37, 42–43
Luke 18:1–8

# NOVEMBER 15

*"In those days, after that tribulation, the sun will be darkened, and the
moon will not give its light, and the stars will be falling from the sky,
and the powers in the heavens will be shaken.
"And then they will see the 'Son of Man coming in the clouds.'"*
—MARK 13:24–26

As a little girl, I remember listening to our priest talk about
"the day of tribulation." I was terrified that one day I would
see stars fall from the sky and the heavens shaking. But as
an adult, I have a whole new understanding of this
teaching. Like so many others, I have experienced many
days, even years, of tribulation. But in all those lightless
moments, Jesus has made himself known. Though my
world has been shaken, God has come—riding, shining on
clouds of hope. Are you experiencing a day of tribulation?
Look up. God is closer than you think.

Daniel 12:1–3
Psalm 16:5, 8, 9–10, 11 (1)
Hebrews 10:11–14, 18
Mark 13:24–32

# NOVEMBER 16

• ST. MARGARET OF SCOTLAND • ST. GERTRUDE, VIRGIN •

*"What do you want me to do for you?"*
—LUKE 18:41

A blind man has a problem. Even though Jesus is well aware of his need, he asks the man an obvious question: "What do you want me to do for you?" The man expresses his deepest desire: *Lord, please let me see . . .* When the blind man begins having a dialogue with God, healing happens. Today, have a long conversation with God. Ask for his assistance. Tell him what you would like to see happen. Though your needs may be obvious, let God know all that you are hoping for.

1 Maccabees 1:10–15, 41–43, 54–57, 62–63
Psalm 119:53, 61, 134, 150, 155, 158
Luke 18:35–43

*When he reached the place, Jesus looked up and said, "Zacchaeus, come
down quickly, for today I must stay at your house."*
—LUKE 19:5

Zaccheaus was a despised tax collector, notorious for
cheating the public. But when Jesus came to town,
Zaccheaus did something brazen. He climbed a tree. I can
just imagine people in the crowd looking up and saying,
"There's that guy who cheated us. Who does he think he
is?" Jesus looks up too. But he sees someone who needs
love and forgiveness. He offers the tax collector time and
friendship. In turn, Zaccheaus experiences a conversion of
heart. This week, reach out to those you resent.

2 Maccabees 6:18–31
Psalm 3:2–3, 4–5, 6–7
Luke 19:1–10

# NOVEMBER 18

• THE DEDICATION OF THE BASILICAS OF SS. PETER AND PAUL, APOSTLES • ST. ROSE-PHILIPPINE DUCHESNE, VIRGIN •

*He replied, "Well done, good servant!"*
—LUKE 19:17

The other day, a colleague mentioned that I had done a great job on a project. He offered his encouragement as he rushed past my office on his way to a meeting. The little affirmation, offered in passing, made my day. When we take the time to affirm our family, friends, and coworkers, we share a powerful gift. One supportive comment can banish a hundred negative remarks.

2 Maccabees 7:1, 20–31
Psalm 17:1bcd, 5–6, 8b and 15
Luke 19:11–28

# NOVEMBER 19

*As Jesus drew near Jerusalem, he saw the city and wept over it.*
—LUKE 19:41

We all have a different image of God. To some people God might be a friend or miracle worker. Others might see him as an all-consuming fire, a presence to be feared. Many don't believe that God exists. In today's Gospel, Jesus is crying. We can't know for certain why—maybe he was overcome by the miseries that waited for him in Jerusalem. He would die there, on a cross. But maybe he was crying for us. Maybe in that emotive moment, Jesus realized that we were worth dying for. If you feel estranged from God, or doubtful of his existence, reflect upon the image of a weeping Christ.

1 Maccabees 2:15–29
Psalm 50:1b–2, 5–6, 14–15
Luke 19:41–44

*But they could find no way to accomplish their purpose because all the*
*people were hanging on his words.*
—LUKE 19:48

Yesterday, I watched a long television infomercial. As the
program began, a businessman packed veggies into a
high-powered blender. "This little machine can decimate
concrete," he said. The camera panned over the audience.
Dozens of nicely dressed people shook their heads in
amazement, their eyes wide. They hung on the blender
man's every word. For a moment I actually thought of
ordering the product. But I realized I was being swayed by
the man's convictions, not mine. *My blender is just fine*, I
thought. Whose words do I hang on? Who holds the most
sway in my life?

1 Maccabees 4:36–37, 52–59
1 Chronicles 29:10bcd, 11abc, 11d–12a, 12bcd
Luke 19:45–48

# NOVEMBER 21

*"Now at the resurrection whose wife will that woman be?"*
—LUKE 20:33

When my daughter Sarah was a teenager, she often talked about Michael, her "true love." Michael was an autistic boy in her special education class. One morning, as we ate breakfast at the kitchen table, Sarah told us that she was going to marry Michael. The eyes of her two younger sisters grew wide. They knew, as I did, that Sarah could never live on her own. Then Rachael, my youngest spoke up: "Sarah, if you got married, we'd miss you." Sarah smiled and said, "I changed my mind. I want to stay with my family." In heaven, there won't be any need for marriage. As we gather with our eternal family, we will be bonded by a love that is greater, stronger, deeper, than any love we have known on the earth. We will see God—our one true love.

1 Maccabees 6:1–13
Psalm 9:2–3, 4 and 6, 16 and 19
Luke 20:27–40

# NOVEMBER 22

*"But as it is, my kingdom is not here."*
—JOHN 18:36

Imelda Marcos was the wife of Ferdinand Marcos, former president of the Philippines. She had 2,700 pairs of shoes. When her husband was ousted from office in 1986, newscasters began reporting on Imelda's extravagant shoe collection. At that time, I was a young mom. I remember thinking, "Wow! What would it be like to have so many shoes?" But I don't envy Imelda. When we leave this earth, we can't pack a suitcase filled with our extravagant belongings. We can't take our shoes, clothes, houses, or cars. We can only bring our cherished memories, our faith, and our trust in God.

Daniel 7:13–14
Psalm 93:1, 1–2, 5 (1a)
Revelation 1:5–8
John 18:33B–37

# NOVEMBER 23

• ST. CLEMENT I, POPE AND MARTYR • ST. COLUMBAN, ABBOT • BLESSED
MIGUEL AGUSTIN PRO, PRIEST AND MARTYR •

*To these four young men God gave knowledge and proficiency in all
literature and science, and to Daniel the understanding of all
visions and dreams.*
—DANIEL 1:17

Every Saturday morning, at quarter to eight, I attend a
speech improvement class. There are about fifteen of us
who gather at that early morning hour. Though we come
from different backgrounds, we all want to become better
public speakers. Since I joined the class, I've learned how
important eye contact is. I'm now disciplining myself to
use good hand gestures when I speak. I've mastered the art
of pausing, and I avoid saying, "Ummmm." It's hard work.
But each of us is called to develop our gifts and to become
as proficient as we can in sharing them. Today, think about
the natural skills you've been given. How can you become
more proficient in developing them?

Daniel 1:1–6, 8–20
Daniel 3:52, 53, 54, 55, 56
Luke 21:1–4

# NOVEMBER 24

• ST. ANDREW DUNG-LAC, PRIEST, AND COMPANIONS, MARTYRS •

*He answered, "See that you not be deceived."*
—LUKE 21:8

When I shop for groceries, I read labels, but I've learned that labels can be deceiving. For example, the label on a loaf of bread might read "Made with whole grains." But at closer glance, I'll discover that the primary ingredient is refined flour. Am I that careful about the opinions and teachings I take in? Do I judge them against the truth of Scripture and church teaching?

Daniel 2:31–45
Daniel 3:57, 58, 59, 60, 61
Luke 21:5–11

# NOVEMBER 25

*For I myself shall give you a wisdom in speaking that all your adversaries will be powerless to resist or refute.*
—LUKE 21:15

I know a pastor who always pauses before delivering his Sunday homily. As he stands before his parishioners, he bows his head and utters these words: "Lord may the words of my mouth and the meditations of my heart be pleasing to you" (Psalm 19). His simple prayer is an acknowledgment that he isn't God. God is able to speak through the pastor's humility. We can trust that the right wisdom and words will come to us when we pause and invite God to speak.

Daniel 5:1–6, 13–14, 16–17, 23–28
Daniel 3:62, 63, 64, 65, 66, 67
Luke 21:12–19

*Let the earth bless the Lord.*
—DANIEL 3:74

There's an apartment building that overlooks a busy intersection near my home. Sometimes, when I'm waiting in my car at the stoplight, I'll turn my glance toward a third-floor window. Most of the time, I'll see an older woman looking down at the cars and people that pass by. "Bless her heart," I pray. There's a part of me that feels sorry for her. I wonder if she's lost everyone she's loved. But then again, maybe she is looking down on the world as God does. Perhaps she is pondering the busyness of our lives and wishing more for us. Maybe she is praying, "Bless their hearts."

Daniel 6:12–28
Daniel 3:68, 69, 70, 71, 72, 73, 74
Luke 21:20–28

# NOVEMBER 27

*Heaven and earth will pass away, but my words will not pass away.*
—LUKE 21:33

When someone dies, we often say that they "passed away." The phrase softens the blow and helps us come to terms with our loss. But as believers, we know that our loved ones haven't really passed away. We can trust that a great resurrection has come. They are with us, "the saints triumphant," cheering us on from heaven. So, too, God's word can never die. When we read or listen to the Scriptures, the Lord breathes life into dying hearts. Today, spend some time reading the words that *will not pass away*. Let God raise you to new life.

Daniel 7:2–14
Daniel 3:75, 76, 77, 78, 79, 80, 81
Luke 21:29–33

# NOVEMBER 28

*Be vigilant at all times.*
—LUKE 21:36

One winter, my three little girls had strep throat at the
same time. For about a week, I was quarantined in our
home. Day and night, I kept a vigil by their bedsides. I put
cool washcloths on their foreheads. I fed them soup and
read them stories. I watched them when they slept.
Though I sometimes grew weary, I wanted them to feel
loved. All these years later, I look back and say, "That was a
special time." Jesus tells us that we must be vigilant at all
times. Day and night, we are called to notice those who
are hungry, sick, and poor.

Daniel 7:15–27
Daniel 3:82, 83, 84, 85, 86, 87
Luke 21:34–36

# NOVEMBER 29

• FIRST SUNDAY OF ADVENT •

*Brothers and sisters: May the Lord make you increase and abound in love for one another and for all, just as we have for you.*
—1 THESSALONIANS 3:12

The readings for today remind us that our love should increase for one another. Today, think about the most important relationships in your life. How can you bring more love into your home, your job, and your community of faith?

Jeremiah 33:14–16
Psalm 25:4–5, 8–9, 10, 14 (1b)
1 Thessalonians 3:12–4:2
Luke 21:25–28, 34–36

# NOVEMBER 30

• ST. ANDREW, APOSTLE •

*If you confess with your mouth that Jesus is Lord and believe in your*
*heart that God raised him from the dead, you will be saved.*
—ROMANS 10:9

Each day we are given opportunities to confess our faith to
the world. Often, our confession of faith is spoken without
words. When we share a smile or a small kindness, we are
proclaiming the goodness of God. Today, be kind. It's a
wonderful way to tell others about Christ.

Romans 10:9–18
Psalm 19:8, 9, 10, 11
Matthew 4:18–22

# DECEMBER 1

*The baby shall play by the cobra's den.*
—ISAIAH 11:8

Young moms and dads go to great lengths to shield their babies from harm. But imagine a world in which children never get hurt or sick and wild animals pose no threat. Envision a place where no one is bullied or battered or broken. That's what God has ready for us.

Isaiah 11:1–10
Psalm 72:1–2,7–8,12–13,17
Luke 10:21–24

*Jesus said to them, "How many loaves do you have?"*
—MATTHEW 15:29–37

Today's Gospel is a reminder that a little gift can go a long way. Today, use your humble skills and talents to the best of your ability. Let God multiply what you already have.

Isaiah 25:6–10a
Psalm 23:1–3a, 3b–4, 5, 6
Matthew 15:29–37

# DECEMBER 3

• ST. FRANCIS XAVIER, PRIEST •

*The rain fell, the floods came, and the winds blew and buffeted the*
*house. But it did not collapse; it had been set solidly on rock.*
—MATTHEW 7:25

Some of the homes in our neighborhood are more than a
hundred years old. The houses have charming details:
screened porches, stained-glass windows, and old wooden
floors. The bungalows and Dutch colonials were built with
strong foundations and have survived decades of snow,
wind, and rain. So, too, God wants us to weather the years.
If we build our faith on him, our house will stand.

Isaiah 26:1–6
Psalm 118:1 and 8–9, 19–21, 25–27a
Matthew 7:21, 24–27

*But a very little while, / and Lebanon shall be changed into an*
*orchard, / and the orchard be regarded as a forest.*
—ISAIAH 29:17

Sometimes it's easy to think that the hardships of life will never change. When we go through an illness or a time of grieving, it's hard to imagine that we will ever be happy again. But the snow of winter always melts away. With God's grace, our lives might be healed when we least expect it. Today, remember to be hopeful. A change might be right around the corner.

Isaiah 29:17–24
Psalm 27:1, 4, 13–14
Matthew 9:27–31

*Saturday*

# DECEMBER 5

*He will be gracious to you when you cry out, / as soon as he hears he will answer you.*
—ISAIAH 30:19

Sometimes it seems that our conversations with God are one-sided. Most of us have wondered if God is even listening to our prayers. But the Scriptures promise that God hears the cries of our hearts. In his own way and time, he will answer our pleas.

Isaiah 30:19–21, 23–26
Psalm 147:1–2, 3–4, 5–6
Matthew 9:35–10:1, 5a, 6–8

# DECEMBER 6

*"A voice of one crying out in the desert: / 'Prepare the way of the Lord, / make straight his paths.'"*
—LUKE 3:4

Moses was called to the desert for forty years. In the dry, desolate wasteland, he met God. Though the landscape was lifeless, God spoke to Moses and gave him directions for the next part of life. Are you in a desert place? Maybe God has something to share with you.

Baruch 5:1–9
Psalm 126:1–2, 2–3, 4–5, 6 (3)
Philippians 1:4–6, 8–11
Luke 3:1–6

# DECEMBER 7

• ST. AMBROSE, BISHOP AND DOCTOR OF THE CHURCH •

*"What are you thinking in your hearts? Which is easier, to say, 'Your sins are forgiven,' or to say, 'Rise and walk'?"*
—LUKE 5:22

It's difficult to forgive those who have harmed us. But when we refuse to let go of our resentment, it's like we are carrying a backpack full of heavy rocks. Jesus doesn't want us to be weighted down with bitterness. If we can't forgive someone on our own, the Lord is always willing to help. With his assistance, we will rise up and walk in freedom.

Isaiah 35:1–10
Psalm 85:9ab and 10, 11–12, 13–14
Luke 5:17–26

# DECEMBER 8

*"Hail, full of grace! The Lord is with you."*
—LUKE 1:28

"The Lord is with you"—Mary heard those words as she
began to recognize her purpose in life. So, too, when we
answer a call to serve Christ, the angels will whisper, "The
Lord is with you."

Genesis 3:9–15, 20
Psalm 98:1, 2–3ab, 3cd–4
Ephesians 1:3–6, 11–12
Luke 1:26–38

*Wednesday*

# DECEMBER 9

*Jesus said to the crowds: "Come to me, all you who labor and are burdened, and I will give you rest."*
—MATTHEW 11:28

After a long day, I often flop onto the couch and watch the nightly news. But it's depressing to hear reports of violence and unrest in the world. Sometimes, I just turn the television off and read the Scriptures. They are good news that brings me rest.

Isaiah 40:25–31
Psalm 103:1–2, 3–4, 8 and 10
Matthew 11:28–30

# DECEMBER 10

*I am the LORD, your God, / who grasp your right hand; / It is I who say to you, "Fear not, / I will help you."*
—ISAIAH 41:13

Do you need assistance with something today? Ask God to intervene. Imagine him grasping your right hand. Hear him say, "Fear not, I will help you."

*Friday*

# DECEMBER 11

• ST. DAMASUS I, POPE •

*I, the LORD, your God, / teach you what is for your good, / and lead you on the way you should go.*
—ISAIAH 48:17

Think of the best teacher you have had. What was it that drew you to that person? In what ways did he or she influence you, and how was your life changed because of it? As you remember your teacher, call to mind all the ways in which God has tutored you.

Isaiah 48:17–19
Psalm 1:1–2, 3, 4 and 6
Matthew 11:16–19

# DECEMBER 12

• OUR LADY OF GUADALUPE •

*Sing and rejoice, O daughter Zion! See, I am coming to dwell among*
*you, says the LORD.*
—ZECHARIAH 2:14

In the opening scene of the movie *The Sound of Music*, Julie
Andrews is dancing and singing on a scenic mountaintop.
Underneath the blue sky, her arms are outstretched. It's as
if joy has raptured her heart and she cannot contain
herself. Have you have felt this kind of happiness? Have
you experienced the joy of God's presence?

Zechariah 2:14–17 or Revelation 11:19a;
12:1–6a, 10ab
Judith 13:18bcde, 19
Luke 1:26–38 or 1:39–47

*On that day, it shall be said to Jerusalem: / Fear not, O Zion, be not
discouraged! / The LORD, your God, is in your midst, /
a mighty savior.*
—ZEPHANIAH 3:14

We have good days and bad days. When we experience
the difficult days, it's hard to imagine that our struggles
will pass. But the prophet Zephaniah reminds us that
things can and will get better. We need not be afraid or
discouraged. Good days will come again.

Zephaniah 3:14–18a
Isaiah 12:2–3, 4, 5–6 (6)
Philippians 4:4–7
Luke 3:10–18

*In your kindness remember me, / because of your goodness, O LORD.*
—PSALM 25

How do you imagine God? Do you see him as a bearded judge ready to condemn your sins? Is he an all-consuming fire, unapproachable? Today, try imagining God as a parent with open arms. No matter how unworthy you feel, remember that God is kind and good.

Numbers 24:2–7, 15–17a
Psalm 25:4–5ab, 6 and 7bc, 8–9
Matthew 21:23–27

# DECEMBER 15

*Jesus said to them, "Amen, I say to you, tax collectors and prostitutes
are entering the Kingdom of God before you."*
—MATTHEW 21:38

It's easy to judge people by their appearance. Prostitutes
are often judged for wearing seductive clothing and heavy
makeup. But who can ever know the circumstances that
forced them to the streets? Jesus always sees beyond
appearances. He knows the secrets of every heart.

Zephaniah 3:1–2, 9–13
Psalm 34:2–3, 6–7, 17–18, 19 and 23
Matthew 21:28–32

# DECEMBER 16

*At that time, Jesus cured many of their diseases, sufferings, and evil spirits; he also granted sight to many who were blind.*
—LUKE 7:21

We all experience spiritual blindness. When we refuse to see the truth or make a much-needed change, it's as if we are wandering in darkness. In today's reading, Jesus grants sight to the blind. What blindness needs to be healed in your life?

Isaiah 45:6c–8, 18, 21c–25
Psalm 85:9ab and 10, 11–12, 13–14
Luke 7:18b–23

# DECEMBER 17

*May his name be blessed forever.*
—PSALM 72:17

It's amazing to think about how many people, throughout the centuries, have blessed the name of the Lord. In my own family, faith was passed down through three generations. Today, think of your family lineage. Give thanks for the faith of those who came before you.

Genesis 49:2, 8–10
Psalm 72:1–2, 3–4ab, 7–8, 17
Matthew 1:1–17

*For it is through the Holy Spirit that this child has been
conceived in her.*
—MATTHEW 1:20

What is the Holy Spirit conceiving in your life? Are you
saying yes to the new birth?

*The woman bore a son and named him Samson. The boy grew up and the LORD blessed him; the Spirit of the LORD stirred him.*
—JUDGES 13:25

Have you ever experienced the Lord "stirring" your heart?
Are you being prompted to make a huge change in
your life?

Judges 13:2–7, 24–25a
Psalm 71:3–4a, 5–6ab, 16–17
Luke 1:5–25

*Mary set out and traveled to the hill country in haste.*
—LUKE 1:39

Sometimes we are called to wait upon God. Other times, we must move "in haste," as Mary did. Today, think about the call God makes in your life. Are you being instructed to wait? Or is it time to move in haste?

Micah 5:1–4a
Psalm 80:2–3, 15–16, 18–19 (4)
Hebrews 10:5–10
Luke 1:39–45

# DECEMBER 21

• ST. PETER CANISIUS, PRIEST AND DOCTOR OF THE CHURCH •

*The flowers appear on the earth, / the time of pruning has come, / and the song of the dove is heard in our land.*
—SONG OF SONGS 2:11

We can go through long winters, but spring always comes. God promises us that flowers will bloom once again. If you are shivering through a wintry time of soul, close your eyes. Imagine the warmth to come.

Song of Songs 2:8–14 or Zephaniah 3:14–18a
Psalm 33:2–3, 11–12, 20–21
Luke 1:39–45

# DECEMBER 22

*"My soul proclaims the greatness of the Lord."*
—LUKE 1:46

When Mary proclaimed the greatness of the Lord, there
was probably great conviction in her voice. I can imagine
her standing straight and tall with her head held high. I see
her with arms raised to heaven. Today, try proclaiming, out
loud, the greatness of the Lord. Turn your glance toward
heaven and hold your head high.

1 Samuel 1:24–28
1 Samuel 2:1, 4–5, 6–7, 8abcd
Luke 1:46–56

*All who heard these things took them to heart, saying, "What, then, will this child be?" For surely the hand of the Lord was with him.*
—LUKE 1:66

When God leads us, we experience anticipation. Though we may not know what lies ahead, we can trust that God's hand is upon us. As with the people in today's reading, thoughts of the future may seem overwhelming. Still, we can rejoice that God will guide our path.

Malachi 3:1–4, 23–24
Psalm 25:4–5ab, 8–9, 10 and 14
Luke 1:57–66

# DECEMBER 24

*"In the tender compassion of our God, / the dawn from on high shall
break upon us, / to shine on those who dwell in darkness and the
shadow of death, / and to guide our feet into the way of peace."*
—LUKE 1:79

Today, imagine the sun rising over the darkness that
shadows your day. Feel the warm rays of God's presence
shining upon you. Let yourself feel calm and peaceful.
All is well.

MORNING:
2 Samuel 7:1–5, 8b–12, 14a, 16
Psalm 89:2–3, 4–5, 27 and 29
Luke 1:67–79

*See, the LORD proclaims / to the ends of the earth: / say to daughter Zion, / your savior comes!*
—ISAIAH 62:11

## On this blessed Christmas Day, how does your Savior come to you?

VIGIL:
Isaiah 62:1–5
Psalm 89:4–5, 16–17, 27, 29 (2a)
Acts 13:16–17, 22–25
Matthew 1:1–25 or 1:18–25

DURING THE NIGHT:
Isaiah 9:1–6
Psalm 96:1–2, 2–3, 11–12, 13
Titus 2:11–14
Luke 2:1–14

DAWN:
Isaiah 62:11–12
Psalm 97:1, 6, 11–12
Titus 3:4–7
Luke 2:15–20

DAY:
Isaiah 52:7–10
Psalm 98:1, 2–3, 3–4, 5–6 (3c)
Hebrews 1:1–6
John 1:1–18 or 1:1–5, 9–14

# DECEMBER 26

• ST. STEPHEN, THE FIRST MARTYR •

*"Behold, I see the heavens opened and the Son of Man standing at the right hand of God."*
—ACTS 7:55

St. Stephen witnessed a glorious image of Jesus. How do you see him? What does his face look like? What message does he speak to you?

Acts 6:8–10; 7:54–59
Psalm 31:3cd–4, 6 and 8ab, 16bc and 17
Matthew 10:17–22

# DECEMBER 27

• THE HOLY FAMILY OF JESUS, MARY, AND JOSEPH •

*Beloved, see what love the Father has bestowed upon us that we may be called the children of God.*

—1 JOHN 3:1

Today, open your eyes and see what love God has bestowed upon your life.

Sirach 3:2–6, 12–14 or 1 Samuel 1:20–22, 24–28
Psalm 84:2–3, 5–6, 9–10 or Psalm 128:1–2, 3, 4–5
Colossians 3:12–21 or 3:12–17 or
1 John 3:1–2, 21–24
Luke 2:41–52

# DECEMBER 28

• THE HOLY INNOCENTS, MARTYRS •

*But if anyone does sin, we have an Advocate with the Father, Jesus
Christ the righteous one.*
—1 JOHN 2:1

When we sin, it's never a permanent break with God.
Today's reading reminds us that Jesus is our advocate. His
mercy is far greater than we can imagine. If you are bound
by a sin in your life, know that Jesus is nearer than you
think. Receive his forgiveness. Be free.

1 John 1:5–2:2
Psalm 124:2–3, 4–5, 7b–8
Matthew 2:13–18

# DECEMBER 29

• ST. THOMAS BECKET, BISHOP AND MARTYR •

*Whoever says, "I know him," but does not keep his commandments is a liar, and the truth is not in him.*
—1 JOHN 2:4

We are called to keep the commandments of God. Fortunately, when we break these sacred mandates, God bestows upon us his abundant grace and forgiveness. Today, celebrate the mercy of Christ. Live your faith as best you can and be truthful in living out your call. God is in you.

1 John 2:3–11
Psalm 96:1–2a, 2b–3, 5b–6
Luke 2:22–35

# DECEMBER 30

*Yet the world and its enticement are passing away. But whoever does the
will of God remains forever.*
—1 JOHN 2:17

Seeking God's will requires discipline. If we want to
discover God's plan, it's important to pray and meditate on
the Scriptures. It's also crucial to seek the guidance of
trusted friends and professionals. How are you seeking
God's will for your life?

1 John 2:12–17
Psalm 96:7–8a, 8b–9, 10
Luke 2:36–40

# DECEMBER 31

• ST. SYLVESTER I, POPE •

*From his fullness we have all received, grace in place of grace.*
—JOHN 1:16

God does not put a cap on grace but pours it out, lavishly,
upon us. Today, stand in this abundant rainfall.

# About the Author

Nancy Jo Sullivan is the author of five books, including *Small Mercies: Glimpses of God in Everyday Life*, and is a frequent speaker at both the local and national levels. She is a columnist for two websites: *Catholic Exchange* and *Catholic Mom*. Sullivan lives in St. Paul, Minnesota.

# More Inspirational Titles from Loyola Press

**Daily Inspiration for Women**
Seasons of a Woman's Life

$12.95 | PB | 4041-6

**Wholehearted Living**
Five-Minute Reflections
for Modern Moms

$13.95 | PB | 4054-6

**An Ignatian Book of Days**

$12.95 | PB | 4145-1

**TO ORDER:** Call 800.621.1008, visit loyolapress.com/store, or visit your local bookseller.

# Continue the Conversation

If you enjoyed this book, then connect with Loyola Press to continue the conversation, engage with other readers, and find out about new and upcoming books from your favorite spiritual writers.

Visit us at **LoyolaPress.com** to create an account and register for our newsletters.

Or scan the code to the left with your smartphone.

---

Connect with us through:

 **Facebook** facebook.com /loyolapress

 **Twitter** twitter.com /loyolapress

 **YouTube** youtube.com /loyolapress

# Preorder Now for a 25% Discount!

Deepen your connection with God and fill each day with grace! Order your 2016 edition of *A Book of Grace-Filled Days* today and **SAVE 25%** by using the promo code **4471**.

Not valid with other offers. Shipping and handling are additional. U.S. domestic orders only. Limited time offer. Valid while supplies last. Offer expires 12/31/2015.